Net Prophet
The Bill Garrett Story

By
Hetty Gray

Net Prophet

The Bill Garrett Story

Copyright © 2001 by Hetty Gray

Library of Congress Control Number 2001 132911
ISBN 0-9712571-0-8

Printed in the United States of America

First Edition

Published by
SUGAR CREEK PUBLISHING
Fairland, IN
www.sugarcreekpublishing.com

Produced by
PPC BOOKS
Redington Shores, FL

To William Leon Garrett
1929-1974

Preface

1946 — early autumn. You hurry out the door and climb into the black 1939 Ford two-door. As you back out of the narrow one-car, clapboard garage and drive down the alley, you glance at your watch. You should have plenty of time. You turn into the street and head toward the south end of town. As you round the curve below the Ewing Mortuary on South Harrison Street, you notice more traffic than usual. After a quick right onto Jefferson Avenue, you spot people walking west from hurriedly parked cars.

The sound of the motor drowns out your frustrated comments. Luckily, a car pulls away from a generous parking place on the south side of 1st Street. Encouraged by the lucky break, you gingerly swing the car over to the curb, and parallel park.

As you climb out of the car, you stop an instant and smooth your clothes that rumpled a bit as you slid across the heavy cloth upholstery. The thud of your driver's door mingles with similar sounds up and down the narrow street. You hurry along the sidewalk and join a throng of others as they walk first west, south, and then west again. Just as you round the last corner, you halt and take a breath.

A line. Again. You based your timing on last year, but leaving earlier hasn't helped a bit. A sea of humanity spills from the triple doors at the top of the stairs on the north face of the building and marches across the broad ribbon of pale

i

gray pavement between the tiers of steps leading toward the footway abutting 2nd Street. The first section of the school path ends at the first five steps. Next, a second, longer expanse of concrete bisects the sloping lawn and ends at the last eight steps leading up into the main entrance.

Men's hats dot the crowd. Literally hundreds of people wait passively in front of the imposing, three-story brick. The doors are wide open and expose a yawning, dark hole through which a trickle of people comes and goes.

Above the doors tower three massive, eighteen-paned windows. Two impressive Ionic, limestone columns support a heavy stone lentil, upon which are chiseled two words: HIGH SCHOOL. Below those words, the line files into the building, one or two at a time.

Shelbyville High School stands before you this morning much as it did on its opening day, January 1, 1912. Your town takes understandable pride in the sprawling complex. The main building, a large, three-story edifice, houses both the junior and senior high schools.

Although no physical barrier exists between the two sections, each student recognizes that the southeast jog in the hallways marks the boundary line between the two levels of education.

A long, rectangular bicycle shed sits behind the one-story boiler room attached to the southwest side of the main building. An expansive structure, its shingled roof offers shelter for those riders who arrive in time to get their bicycles under cover on a first-come, first-served basis. Outside, another two pairs of wood racks afford students more space, although exposed to the elements. Passersby recognize the bicycle shed as a popular common gathering place for hundreds of students, both before and after classes.

As far as the wider community is concerned, however,

the true Mecca lies a bit further south, in the form of a large, brick gymnasium. This building seats up to 2,200 persons and commands the south edge of the block bounded by 2nd, 3rd, Tompkins, and Meridian Streets. Entry into the facility is the primary concern that weighs heavily on the minds of those around you.

Why? Because the goal of each man and woman in the line is equal to yours: to purchase a portion of those seats as season tickets. Although four varsity sports comprise the high school boys' athletic schedule, true to Indiana tradition, basketball reigns supreme.

You observe the horde carefully. Moving at a snail's pace, fans chat among themselves. Conversations are jumbled, but excited in tone. Some people highlight the most exciting games from last season, while others trumpet inspired hopes for the upcoming one. Here, assembled politely in a queue for the hottest ticket in town, the group absolutely mesmerizes you.

The fall weather cooperates nicely this morning. Few wear coats, and, as you scan the assembled mob, you note that their attire accurately mirrors a portrait of the city's demographics.

Ahead of you, a group of men huddles together, dressed in factory uniforms. Their first names are embroidered on their shirts beneath a much larger pronouncement of a company name. Further behind you stands a completely different genre of working men. These men constantly shift their weight from one foot to another. Clad in suits and ties, they appear staid and patient, but, every now and then, you watch as one of them pulls up a coat sleeve or reaches into a pocket to check the time. Their offices wait.

The variety is solidly Hoosier — collared clergy, factory workers, professional men, housewives, retirees, and young parents with children in tow. Pre-schoolers fidget and tug a pant leg or a dress hem in understandable frustration. Minutes loom as an eternity to a three-year-old. You smile as you watch mothers bend down to console their toddlers. The colorful mix of humanity surges ahead of you as it inches its way toward the top of those last eight concrete steps.

Once inside, the line creeps across the hall and ascends the broad, metal hand railed east staircase that abuts the two-story, floor to ceiling windows along the entire north wall of a huge assembly room, the virtual heart of the main building. Students sit below you in neat rows of wooden desks with folding seats. Wide aisles divide the large study hall into sections. Here and there, a youngster glances up toward you and the other fans.

Your vantage point offers you an excellent view of the entire hall. You reflect on the group. Many students pore over textbooks and notes. In the back of the room, a tall girl checks an atlas on a large stand. But, there is something amiss there. Something seems odd. A few boys catch your attention. Ah, yes, they are intent on something. You can tell. They all concentrate on the teacher in charge. Suddenly, a volley of white peppers the air, and sundry students react in response to a very unexpected rear assault.

You laugh to yourself and turn away. You see no point in encouraging the rascals by giving them a sympathetic audience. After all, it hasn't been that long since you sat in the same room. It's the same old game. Armed with their small, white weapons, the mischievous boys watch for just the right moment to launch a well-formed spitball at a carefully selected target several rows of desks away. No matter how much things change, they stay the same. Alas, boys will forever be boys.

The bell rings. Students scurry in and out of the study

hall. The cacophony of mirthful enthusiasm drifts through the windows toward you. Giggles fill the halls as clots of girls try to catch up on the latest news as they scamper toward their next classes. Meanwhile, the press of basketball fans waits to step onto the third floor and walk the final fifteen or so feet to the health department. There, inside the narrow, tiered lecture halls — one for the boys and one for the girls, of course, — sit the tables of the all-powerful ticket sellers.

Twenty minutes after you take that last step onto the third floor, you descend the stairs and grin at those in line behind you. You clutch your precious season tickets to your chest as you sidle outside. You handle them with care. They look better today than they ever will. No punch holes perforate the unwrinkled cardboard. As you walk toward the car, a cool breeze plays through your hair and the odd, stale scent of dried fall leaves perfumes the air.

The weather knows. The wind swells among the tops of the giant trees along Elm Street, and its sound mimics the hoarse crescendo of the fans, soon to fill the high school gym. You love the frenzied sounds of the hometown crowd. In your opinion, the seven-month hiatus since the last time you heard that roar seems like years. You can't wait for that first home game when you sit down on the bleachers to revel in what is a treasured Hoosier tradition — the competitive, exhilarating thrill of Indiana high school basketball.

Reflections from Present Day Shelbyville

Today, one finds it hard to imagine that a good proportion of a city's workforce would sacrifice a partial day's pay to wait in line for high school basketball season tickets. But, as a matter of fact, during the 1940s and 1950s, the local workers did just that. Characteristically, Shelbyville was not unique in that regard. Similar ticket lines replicated themselves across the state. In most cases, if fans didn't get in line on the first day of ticket sales, they missed out on their preferred seats. As any "true blue" Indiana basketball fan of that era would affirm, seat choice ranked as the "number one" consideration, above all else. The facility's seating preferences differed, yet, one thing was certain — Shelbyville's Paul Cross Gym offered its fans a wide selection.

Narrow bleachers rose from the flawless hardwood floor to the rafters. Seating climbed at a low angle toward the row of metal-paned windows banding the structure's east and west walls. Sharp, teepee shaped passageways provided the athletic department badly needed weight areas and storage niches beneath the bleachers. The staff took advantage of every available square foot of space for odd trunks of athletic paraphernalia and off-season equipment. Efficient use of space beneath the seating areas left the four inside corners of the structure completely open for concession stands and entryways.

A stage dominated the north end of the gym, and a one-story section the width of the building, east to west, housed the music and industrial arts departments, positioning both band and the choir rooms directly behind the stage. The coaches' offices flanked the stage, and stairs on either side descended to the basement. The west stairs led to public restrooms, while the east stairs led to companion locker rooms for the home team and the visitors. Inside, the four sides of the gym resembled any number of its counterparts during the 1940s, yet, uniquely, Shelbyville's gym featured perhaps the most unusual corner seating areas in central Indiana. Each of these sections sat one level up, tucked high over each corner of the playing floor.

Known as "the crow's nests" by some fans, and as "pigeon roosts" by others, these triangular seating areas offered a panoramic view of the excellent hardwood court that ran north and south. Some fans stubbornly refused to sit anywhere else. The widest was the first row, and then each succeeding row shortened, until only one seat remained at the apex of the section. From any three of those four areas, the fans could survey the gymnasium with ease. The southwest corner section was reserved for the high school band.

Banners hung high along the walls, nearly at ceiling level. The brightly colored pennants proclaimed each tournament title and year in which it was won. Golden Bear fans took great pride in those banners. Yet, no matter how many conference, sectional, and regional victory banners hung in the building, the crowd hungered for one designation alone — State Champions.

Looking back, Shelbyville's Paul Cross Gym shone as a microcosm of small-town, Heartland America in an era when its love for the sport of basketball overarched all high school sports. In truth, that era exemplified the pinnacle of basketball fever in the State of Indiana.

It was in The Paul Cross Gymnasium, certainly judged Spartan by today's standards, that a young man named William Leon Garrett honed his athletic skills. It was within the wide halls of Shelbyville Jr.-Sr. High School that he forged deep friendships with his classmates. It was under the tutelage of a staff of exemplary teachers and dedicated coaches that he excelled in the classroom, upon the track, across the baseball diamond, and on the basketball court. The support of a loving, close family grounded him. Throughout his life, his persona remained the same. He was, from youth, an extraordinary human being. This, then, is his story.

Author's Note

William Leon Garrett's life spanned far more than the twenty-five feet between the "top of the key" and the goal on the basketball court. In his forty-five years, Bill not only broke the racial barrier in The Big Ten Conference, but he also left an unmistakable legacy, a legacy merited over many years by his quiet demeanor and an ingrained, determined sense of fairness.

To judge his life simply within the confines of stripes painted on a glistening hardwood floor is to ignore the character of a man who lived far too few years. Despite the fact that we may never know what he could have given the young people of Indiana had he lived, we can appreciate his stellar accomplishments and assign him his rightful place as a cherished Hoosier.

Acknowledgements

I would like to personally thank all those persons who made personal contributions to this book. In the course of my research on Bill Garrett, I spoke with people of legendary caliber in Indiana. The value of their input is incalculable.

Special thanks are due to Betty Guess Garrett Inskeep, whose clear memory succinctly recalls every imaginable detail of Bill's personal life as an adult. Also, I wish to thank Bill's brother and sisters for their glimpses into their older brother's childhood, and Bill and Betty's four children, Tina Louise, Judith Ann, Laurie Jean, and William Guess Garrett for their memories of their father.

The following persons and organizations merit my thanks for their help in research efforts: The Kentucky Historical Society Research Collections; Kathy Jacobs, Community Relations Director, Oldham County Chamber of Commerce, LaGrange, Kentucky; June Barnett, The Grover Museum, Shelbyville, Indiana; James Sleeth; Sponsel/Dillman Photography; Ray Ewick, Director of The Indiana State Library; Louis "Gene" Byrd; Pauline Scott; Bonnie Lundin; The Second Baptist Church of Shelbyville, Indiana; The Shelbyville-Shelby County Public Library; Jeff Brown, Sports Editor, *The Shelbyville News*; David Craig, Historical Columnist, *The Shelbyville News*; Ron Hamilton, Guest Columnist, *The Shelbyville News*; Bob Gordon, Curator, The Robert Brandt Photography Collection; Maureen Sheehan, Genealogy Librarian, The Shelbyville-Shelby County Public Library; Dr. Clifton Latshaw, retired veterinarian and Shelbyville history specialist; Brad Cook, Indiana University Archives; Mae Sampanis, Assistant to President Miles Brand, Indiana University, Bloomington, Indiana; *The Indiana Daily Student* Archives, Indiana University; Diane Hanson, Microforms Supervisor, Indiana University Main Library; *Bloomington Herald Times* Archives, Monroe County Public Library, Bloomington; Connie Wampler, University Alumni Services, Bloomington; Judy Schroeder, The Indiana University Alumni Association, Bloomington; B. J. McElroy, Indiana University Athletic Department; Kim Dunning, Indiana University Media Relations; *The Indianapolis Star-News* Archives, The Indianapolis-Marion County Public Library, Indianapolis, Indiana; Laurie Miller, 82nd Street Kinko's, Indianapolis; Eric Simonelli, Public Relations, The Boston Celtics, Boston, Massachusetts; Govoner Vaughn, Archivist, The Harlem Globetrotters, Phoenix, Arizona; Marie Lawlor, Indianapolis Public Schools; Carole Wilburn, City of Indianapolis' Metropolitan Plan Commission; Nancy, Mayor's Action Center, City of Indianapolis ; Angie Stewart and Sean Price, Indianapolis Police Department, North District; Shelley Tyler, President, Indianapolis Chapter, Crispus Attucks Alumni Association; Gilbert Taylor, Director, The Crispus Attucks Museum, Indianapolis, Indiana; Lorna Webb, Crispus Attucks Multi-Cultural Center Staff; Gary Yohler, Tiffany Photography Studio, Broad Ripple; Ruth Lipscomb, The University of Indianapolis; Rebecca Markel; Blake Ress, Executive Director, and Sports Information Director Jim Russell and his assistant, Jason Willey, The Indiana High School Athletic Association (IHSAA), Indianapolis, Indiana; Bart Kaufman; Richard and Patricia Ewing; Alice Roberson, Rochester, New York; Roger Dickinson, Executive Director, The Indiana Basketball Hall of Fame, New Castle, Indiana; The NCAA, Indianapolis, Indiana; Dr. Gloria King, IVY Tech State College, Indianapolis, Indiana; IUPUI Student Services, Indiana University-Purdue University, Indianapolis, Indiana; Sandra Jones, Providence-St.Mel High School, Chicago, Illinois; and Ted Burger, Macintosh Support, Fairland, Indiana.

Special thanks to Gentron Wintin, wife of the 1947 Shelbyville Police Chief Walter Wintin, and mother of Bill's 1947 Golden Bear teammate, Walter Wintin. She kept a precise record of the entire 1946-47 season, including pre-season predictions and post-season celebrations. Her beautifully kept record chronicled the 1947 campaign in a series of newspaper columns from the opening game to the reviews of the final game.

Informative *Shelbyville Democrat** articles, as well as columns clipped from the major state papers, provided a game by game description of the championship season. However, Gentron's scrapbook may be the only surviving record of the championship team in original condition, because the Shelbyville Sr. High School Library lost its early twentieth century archives cache to water damage several years ago.

I owe my sincere thanks and appreciation to those persons who wrote letters, granted personal interviews, or spoke to me by telephone. They are Herb Schwomeyer, Author of *Hoosier Hysteria*; George Glass and Gerald Scofield who played against and with Bill in grade school basketball; 1947 Golden Bear teammates, Don Robinson, Bill Breck, Loren "Hank" Hemingway, Walter Wintin, and Louis Bower; Ray Ewick, one of Bill's high school track teammates; Clyde Lovellette, retired educator and All-American basketball player at The University of Kansas; Indiana University Hurryin' Hoosiers teammates, Gene Ring, Phil Buck, Bill Tosheff, Lou Watson, and Sam Esposito; IU Hurryin' Hoosiers Senior Team Manager George Vlassis; Ernie Andres, Assistant to IU Head Coach Branch McCracken; James

Roberson, M.D., Bill Garrett's college roommate; George Taliaferro, player, Indiana University's 1945-46 undefeated, Big Ten Championship Football Team; Ray Crowe, former Head Coach and Athletic Director, Crispus Attucks High School, Indianapolis, Indiana; Don Thomas, Bill Garrett's Assistant Basketball Coach at Crispus Attucks High School; Theodore Boyd, Hoosier Author and Poet; Albert Spurlock, Head of Industrial Arts Department and Head Track Coach, Crispus Attucks High School; Edgar Searcy, Crispus Attucks Tiger under Bill Garrett, retired Eli Lilly & Company executive, and practicing attorney in Indianapolis; Barbara Marshall, Shelbyville Sr. High School Athletic Department; Faye "Peachie" Cole, retired assistant to the Shelbyville High School Athletic Director; Harry Larrabee, Head Basketball Coach, The Shelbyville Golden Bears; Steve Downing, Associate Athletic Director, Indiana University; and Mike Davis, Head Coach of the Indiana Hurryin' Hoosiers Basketball Team, Indiana University.

I find it difficult to find the words to express my appreciation to my reviewers. These five men, whose names are "household words" in Indiana basketball, took time to read this book and comment on its content. Highly dedicated individuals, this quintet — not coincidentally a group of five — responded with five unique critiques. Their combined experiences mesh in a delightful series of comments. I am forever in their debt.

Bob King, Department of Intercollegiate Athletics, Purdue University:
Shortridge High School, 1937, Butler University, 1947; coached Basketball & Football 13 years, Shortridge High School, Indianapolis; Original Organizer, Indiana Basketball Coaches' Association.; Chairman, District IV, National High School Coaches' Association.

Dave Nicholson, President, The Indiana Basketball Hall of Fame:
Vallonia (Indiana) High School, 1959; Indiana State University 1965 & 1968; Ball State University, 1978; Coached Indiana high school basketball for 26 years, with four undefeated seasons at Darlington and Noblesville; 3-time Indiana Basketball Coaches' Association Coach of the Year; 16 Coach of the Year Awards; Inductee, The Indiana Basketball Hall of Fame, 1999.

Gene Cato. Former Commissioner, Indiana High School Athletic Association:
Oakland (Indiana) High School, 1949; Oakland City College, 1952; Indiana University, 1956; Indiana State University, 1961; Butler University, 1965; Coach, Principal, and Superintendent of Schools over a 24-year career in Hoosier public education; As IHSAA Commissioner, Cato developed the state tourney system to encompass 17 girls' and boys' sports; Inductee, Indiana Basketball Hall of Fame, 1992.

Sam Alford, Assistant Basketball Coach, The University of Iowa, Iowa City, Iowa:
Washington (Indiana) High School, 1960; Franklin College of Indiana, 1964; Indiana University, 1968; Head Coach, New Castle (Indiana) High School, 1975-1995, with a record of 4 twenty-win seasons; Championships included 14 Sectionals, 6 Regionals, 1 Semi-State, and 3 North Central Conference Titles; Overall home court record — 300 wins and 189 losses.
(Courtesy of Michael Bergurn, Athletic Director, New Castle High School)

Herb Schwomeyer, Color Commentator for WRTV, Indianapolis; Author, *Hoosier Hysteria;* Indiana Basketball Historian:

Indianapolis Manual High School, 1936; B.A. & M.A., Butler University, 1942; Doctorate, Indiana University, 1947; Four-decade career at Butler University, including six years as Tony Hinkle's Assistant Basketball Coach for the Bulldogs; Butler Dean of Men; IHSAA official; Inductee, The Indiana Basketball Hall of Fame, 1974.

*The Shelbyville Democrat existed until December, 1948. After John C. DePrez, Sr. purchased the business, he changed the name to The Shelbyville News.

Chapter One

In 1812, the population of Indiana territory was estimated at around 30,000. Among those tallied, authorities reported, but did not count, several hundred Negroes in the territory. It was a common practice to keep track of Indians and Negroes, but their numbers were not included in the government population totals. Before Indiana gained statehood in 1816, the 30,000 figure would double.

The vast majority of newcomers arrived between 1814 and 1816. These people came mainly from the South, although the New England Yankee, with his strange speech and his sharp eye for a bargain, was already beginning to make an appearance on the Hoosier scene.[1]

From the time land was available for settlement, Negroes owned land in Shelby County, Indiana. County records confirm that a Kentucky slave owner named Thomas Graffort purchased 480 acres in Addison Township. Graffort's Last Will and Testament directed his executor to divide and deed that land to his freed slaves. Shelby County Negro resident George Graffort, holding, in standard pattern, the surname of his owner, came by his 80-acre tract at the probation of Thomas Graffort's estate. Master Graffort hailed from Bourbon County, Kentucky, and it was his wish that those whom he had held as slaves would be owners of their own land after his death.

Very early in the history of Shelby County, nineteenth

century Census records listed Negroes living in the homes of whites. Some Negroes accompanied white families who emigrated from the Eastern Seaboard and the Southern states, but others were actually freedmen, who brought their families to Indiana territory for a better life.

Records and oral family histories traced Bill Garrett's ancestry to antebellum Oldham County, Kentucky. Situated among low rolling hills less than ten miles south of the Ohio River, Oldham County typified an American agricultural area during the last half of the nineteenth century. Oldham County boasted a talented, determined pool of farmers. Tobacco dominated as the main crop, but grain crops added to the bounty. Those commodities not only supplemented the incomes of the area residents, but they also enriched the diets of a wide variety of livestock. The county seat of La Grange, albeit small in population, flourished. Although slavery was common at that time in Kentucky, a number of freedmen and their families lived openly in Oldham County.

Oldham County records attest to a number of male Negro taxpayers in the years preceding the Civil War.[2] However, genealogical research remains difficult for Black Americans who wish to trace their family histories. The explanation is one that aptly describes the tenuous family situations of that time.

Slave auctions wreaked havoc in Negro families. Families were torn apart, physically, and surnames often changed to that of the new owner. As a result, family members had rare opportunities to learn the fates of those from whom they were forcibly separated. Few slaves were literate and no permanent, dependable channels of communication existed from plantation to plantation. Once in a while, word of a family member surfaced unexpectedly; but, alas, to the chagrin of the majority of nineteenth century American slaves, those instances were relatively rare.

Many Kentucky men fought in The Great Civil War. The bulk of them enlisted in Army of the Confederacy, but personal allegiances split families. The bitter conflict pitted brother against brother and father against son. It was not unusual to find family members fighting on opposite sides of the conflict. The ideological schism erupted in house after house across the states bordering the Deep South. Strongly held beliefs and allegiances seeded the bitter feelings that broke asunder many families. In the end, those men loyal to the North left home and enlisted in the Union Army.

Throughout the Civil War, Oldham County residents struggled to maintain daily life with as little disruption as possible. Word of the conflict came "piecemeal," and, more often than not, sources were less than credible. For the soldiers' families, the official military casualty list served as the most reliable authority, but these compilations took a long time to arrive. Consequently, the sudden cessation of letters from the front lines often portended a grisly fate for the soldier in question — husband, father, brother, or son. During the Civil War, the old adage of "No news is good news" did not hold true.

Meanwhile, hundreds of miles north, in Shelby County, Indiana, life mirrored that of Oldham County — to a point. Like her Kentucky counterpart, Shelby County boasted a thriving economy that revolved around agriculture and a smattering of small, commercial businesses located both in and around Shelbyville, the county seat.

The Underground Railroad was a prolific influence in Indiana at that time, and many communities along the Ohio River served as the starting points on a perilous trek toward Canada and freedom. Quakers actively participated in this covert action against Southern slaveowners. Many old Shelby

County stories circulate yet today about just which houses were actually involved in the movement, and some of the purported safe houses still stand. Whites took a stand against slavery, but they were not alone, especially after sentiments led to armed conflict.

Negroes were, by no means, passive onlookers to the Civil War. Citing Benjamin Quarles, in his book, *The Negro in the Civil War*, "to him (the Negro), freedom was a two-way street; indeed he gave prior to receiving. The quarter of a million Negroes north of the Mason-Dixon line, schooled over the years in public affairs by the colored convention movement and the abolitionist crusade, acted as a whip and spur to the administration. In contrast, Negroes in the South were pressed into noncombatant duty, as orderlies and teamsters. Because of such service, these men were constantly under enemy fire. Negro laborers, behind the front lines, threw up the foundations for the artillery, built the forts, and dug the entrenchments. Those slaves who remained at home either manned the factories that sprung up around the South, or they supplied the badly needed brawn for harsh, tireless work in the mines."

The most famous of the Negro regiments in the Union Army was the 54th, honored in the 1989 motion picture, *Glory*. Meanwhile, counterintelligence efforts were ongoing. For example, Kentucky Negro, Henry Blake, worked alone behind enemy lines. Plodding through the woods carefully to avoid detection, Blake provided critical information to the Union Army by spying on Confederate positions a hundred miles below Louisville in 1862. His actions undoubtedly saved many lives. So prolific was Blake that the Stars and Bars placed a bounty of $1,000 on his head.[3]

In that same year, neighboring Ohio had problems of its own. Cincinnati residents feared a Confederate army sweep into their city. Famous Hoosier, General Lew Wallace, later renowned for his book, *Ben Hur*, requested to raise a voluntary brigade of Negroes to throw up defenses for the city. The Negro brigade worked night and day for three weeks. Colonel William M. Dickson lauded the men for their efforts when he presided at a celebration for the six hundred men. The Negro group presented him a sword in recognition for his kindness. Cincinnati residents, like so many of their peers across the North, learned an abject lesson in Negro cooperation in a common cause.[4]

1862 Shelby County records confirm that more than 141 men were drafted into The Union Army. Some of these men belonged to The Union Army's 17th Regiment that marched with General Sherman in his famous thrust "From Atlanta to the Sea."

The Shelby Volunteer newspaper reported all available information, but concentrated, in large part, on details of specific battles. These detailed articles provided little solace to soldiers' families. Wives and children, parents and siblings, bravely hoped and prayed that their loved ones had survived the terrible carnage. However, elapsed time between actual events and their publication only prolonged the heartache for those who agonized over the fates of their men.

The 1830 Shelby County Census documents the fact that white families housed a number of Negroes, especially in the rural areas. However, it must be noted, that neither Indians nor Negroes were included in any official records until after 1840.

Local historians listed Negro resident Michael Fox as the owner of a prosperous blacksmith shop in the original settlement of Little Marion, once touted to be the future county seat. The business operated as The Fox-Kaster Blacksmith shop. Kaster is a very old Shelby County name and it dates back to the earliest settlers. According to genealogy records, *The Republican Banner* newspaper dated March 15th, 1860, chronicled the administration of the Silas Coleman estate. He had worked for the Fox-Kaster shop for many years. Disposition listed his personal effects as a collection of blacksmith tools.

Business began to thrive even before 1865. Enterprises included Switzer's Soap Factory, The Shelby Mills, Sprague's Stave Factory, the Murdock Sawmill, and at least one brickyard.

In the fall of 1861, D. L. Conrey came from Franklin County to Shelbyville, where he would live for the remainder of his life. His business offered furniture, as well as coffins. Today, this seems an odd combination, but 19th century business directories commonly listed "Cabinetmakers and Undertakers" as one category. Fountaintown featured just such a listing on an 1860 Map of Shelby County owned by the author.

Joseph Stewart emigrated from Pennsylvania to Shelby County, Indiana, in 1851. Despite the fact that several of his wood related businesses were destroyed by fire, he rebuilt his companies and eventually partnered in the Stewart and Blakely furniture factory. Over the years, more furniture factories located in Shelbyville, and their owners built some of the most handsome homes in central Indiana.

The furniture business continued to grow in Shelby County, and it attracted German craftsmen, who flocked to the area for stable, good paying jobs. In the off-season, these talented men hand carved elegant trim and woodwork in the sumptuous homes of their company bosses.

At the end of the first year of Shelbyville's founding, both doctors and lawyers had local offices. In addition, most of the smaller towns boasted their own "physician and surgeon." Among those early doctors listed was Benjamin Harrison,

son of William Henry Harrison. According to Masonic records, Dr. Harrison practiced medicine in Shelbyville for about eighteen months before he left for Texas. Some claim that he was killed in the famous Battle of the Alamo.

Dentists, too, settled early into the area. The first listed dentist dated to 1840, when a Dr. G. Lupton set up his practice in the county seat. After he left to serve in the Union Army during the Civil War, other dentists arrived. Charges ranged widely, according to services rendered. For example, tin fillings listed for 50 cents and a full set of teeth in gold priced out at $100.00.[5]

Midwives were common in both the white and Negro communities, but records do not intimate that practicing physicians refused to treat on basis of ethnicity, whether the patient was either a white, a Negro, or an Indian.

In 1868, the Shelby County Census listed resident totals of 41 Negroes and 2,433 whites. By 1904, Negro numbers swelled to 288, and whites to 5,619. These figures included those persons living both inside and outside the city limits of Shelbyville.

Despite the economic similarities shared by Oldham County, Kentucky, and Shelby County, Indiana, the parallel between the two diverged sharply when it came to the subject of how "people of color" were treated.

In Shelbyville, nothing indicated the presence of anti-Negro sentiment. Negro families resided in town prior to the war, and several of them were well-known businessmen. Among these was Dan Morgan. His daughter, Minerva, is believed to be the first Negro child born in the community. Dan was both versatile and popular. He not only managed a famous oyster bar in the Ray House (a local hotel) for a time, but he also owned and operated a barbershop.[6]

No official records confirmed whether or not local Negro

children attended school with their white counterparts prior to 1869. However, in 1869, The Indiana General Assembly passed a law requiring separate schools for "colored children."

Colored citizens responded by organizing a festival to raise funds for the school. The editor of *The Shelby Volunteer* urged the public to patronize the affair. The public response gratified the organizers. The oyster supper raised $200, a large sum compared to other comparable efforts of the time.

During the school year 1869-70, Shelbyville officials built a separate school. Dubbed School No. 2, the "Colored School" cost $3,000. The brick building stood on Harrison Street, one of the town's two main thoroughfares. Built in response to the petition of Second Baptist Church Pastor Miles Bassett, the school's first full academic year was 1870. Coincidentally, 1870 also witnessed famed orator Frederick Douglass speak on "Our Composite Nationality" at Blessing's Opera House (later occupied by the toy department of Shelbyville's century-old J. G. De Prez Hardware store). In 1874, school enrollment stood at 128: 67 boys and 61 girls.[7]

While attendance ratios varied, most sources agree that attendance averaged between 78% and 85% — not only a testament to the school and its staff, but also to parents who placed a high value on education.

According to the 1887 Shelby County History, Negroes in Shelbyville and its vicinity enjoyed few privileges of public worship prior to 1872. The people who came to the area after the Civil War were ill-prepared to pay a pastor or provide themselves with a permanent house of worship.

That scene changed, however, when Robert Watkins arrived in town. At first, he held meetings at his home. Later, through his efforts, supporters founded The African Methodist Episcopal Church in the fall of 1872. Members of the white Methodist Episcopal Church wholeheartedly supported the effort, and the bulk of the $250 cost of the small frame building was borne by the white donors. That degree of sincere concern of whites for their colored neighbors only underscores the degree of cooperation evident between the races for decades before the turn of the century. Sadly, it took far longer for southern populations to achieve such openly amicable relations.

In 1866, other local Negroes founded The Second Baptist Church. Under the sponsorship of six ministers, headed by Reverend William Moore, the fledgling church began on February 19, 1869. The first six years of its existence, the church met on the third floor of a local building. Church officials planned for better quarters. The group saved its money, and, in 1875, they erected a 33 x 50-foot brick building on West Hendricks Street. Second Baptist's congregation grew rapidly from an initial group of seven people in 1869 to more than seventy by 1887.

Decades before the Garrett ancestors migrated from Oldham County, Kentucky, to Shelby County, Indiana, new arrivals found a bustling county seat. The town amazed Southern newcomers. The prospect of concerned white citizens funding and building educational and religious institutions for their Negro neighbors was an exercise in community spirit far disparate from anything they had seen in the South.

The oral family history that linked the Garrett family between Kentucky and Indiana, was confirmed by a family tree that was thoroughly researched by Bill's youngest sister, Laura Mae Garrett Wicks. Laura painstakingly traced her family as far back as Vinnie Price, a hardy woman born about 1854 in LaGrange, Kentucky. She found no record of Vinnie's husband's name, but Vinnie bore him four children.

One daughter, Rachel Price (b. La Grange, 1868), married Allen Wallace (b. LaGrange, 1861). Because no specific details of their movements were found, the exact year of their migration remained an open question.

Chapter Two

Turn of the century Shelby County saw progress for its Negro population. Education continued under the capable hands of Negro instructors, and residents worked side by side with their white counterparts in a number of business and commercial ventures. So highly were county Negro residents respected that court records confirm that local lawyers impaneled an entirely Negro jury in January of 1902. The crime adjudged was a 1901 burglary of a residence belonging to two local men, Robert Smith and George Vaughn.

The culprit was nabbed by the homeowners and held for the authorities. When the jury was seated, each juror, to a person, was a Negro — a "first" in the annals of Shelby County jurisprudence. In contrast to neighboring counties that practiced open bigotry, Shelby County shone as a fine example of even-handed treatment to those of the Negro race.

It was to this county that William Garrett's ancestors emigrated from Kentucky, and the attitudes and practices of whites toward their neighbors, Indian or Negro, lay the foundation for his adult life.

William Leon Garrett, (b. Hodgenville, Kentucky, April 3, 1903) is numbered among the descendants of Rachel Price and Allen Wallace. No written records confirm the exact year the Garrett family moved north to settle in Shelbyville, Indiana, but the community they found was immersed in its efforts toward equal education for all its children, regardless of race.

A good example was the local push for post-secondary education. A college education was not widely sought by a high number of high school graduates, but such degrees were prized. In 1902, The Shelby County Commissioners appointed John Hodge to attend Indiana University at Bloomington, Indiana. He was the first local Negro student to earn such an honor.[8]

Traveling Chautauqua productions and the very popular County Fair provided a wide variety of entertainment for county residents. Among those who spoke at the August, 1912, Chautauqua was Booker T. Washington, a prominent Negro leader and liberal thinker. In addition, 1915 Chautauqua records list Helen Keller and her teacher, Anna Sullivan Macy, as featured speakers. These events were widely attended, and the shows did not restrict admission based on race or gender. However, across the state, even in neighboring counties, bias not only reared its ugly head, but it thrived, whipped into near frenzy by heinous leaders.

Indiana does not stand blameless in terms of bigotry, yet history confirms that the most notorious form of racial bias migrated to the Hoosier State from outside its borders.

In 1922, a man named D.C. Stephenson moved to Indiana from Texas. After losing the nomination for Congress from the district that included Evansville, he emerged as the state's principal organizer of the Ku Klux Klan. A short time after the election, he moved to Indianapolis, where he served as The Grand Dragon of the Klan in Indiana. Speaking from his luxurious suite of offices in the state capital, he proclaimed, "I am the law in Indiana."[9] It was from this central Indiana location that Stephenson, and those who allied with him, began to spread their venomous activity throughout the Hoosier countryside.

In her book, *Biography of a Town*, local author Marian McFadden vividly described the Klan's activities in Shelby County. December of 1922 saw flaming crosses in the county. More were sighted in the Spring of 1923. To the town's shock, in April, a cross burned on the Public Square. The Ku Klux Klan had arrived, and, in May, it organized a parade of members, clad in their signature white sheets.

Only one major event took place that year. In July, Klan organizers staged a "monster" torchlight procession through the streets of Shelbyville. The universal reaction was extremely quiet, and did not please the hooded participants. Instead of prompting cheers and accolades, the marchers found themselves greeted with lines of solemn, silent faces. Despite the fact that the Klan made a deep, and ugly, impression statewide, it failed to enflame the bulk of Shelby County's people. Instead, the hate group only sparked "a short flurry of excitement."[10]

Despite the fact that the overall reaction was one of extreme disapproval, some onlookers questioned the composition of the group. They wondered if any "locals" were involved. There was no sure way to prove that any of the hooded marchers were county men; but, since there had never been trouble of that sort in the community before, authorities held to the firm belief that those who took part in the macabre march were most likely outsiders.

Three years after the Klan tried to gain a foothold in Shelby County, the Garrett family tree produced a new branch. In 1926, Leon Garrett married Laura Belle O'Bannon (b. Shelbyville, Indiana, January 7, 1906). The couple had four children. The eldest, a son, was William Leon Garrett (b. April 4, 1929). Leon held down a good job in the furniture industry.

Local furniture factories first began operation during the mid-1800s, and they flourished by 1900. City records listed twelve operating furniture factories in 1907. However, the outbreak of World War I harshly interrupted the burgeoning economy. One of the first effects of the European conflict was an upsurge in American farm prices. On a local level, people profited, yet, even with the bounty of extra income, the county farmers and city folk found it hard to forget the perils of those in Belgium.

As a result, Shelby County organized drives for funds and clothing to be sent overseas to those in need. Woodrow Wilson won a resounding victory in the 1916 Presidential election. In fact, in retrospect, many of the Wilson votes probably sprang from the Democratic slogan, "He kept us out of war." No doubt, voters hoped that statement would hold true. Alas, it did not. When President Wilson asked Congress to declare war on April 2, 1917, America responded immediately, from the largest metropolis to the smallest town.

In Shelbyville, Indiana, the local Elks Club served as a Red Cross sewing and bandage center. Women of all races and backgrounds participated in the effort. Conscription boards, set up in haste during early June, registered 2,036 men, 123 of whom were called into the service the next month. Liberty bond drives moved the corporate conscience.

War was a reality. Soaring food prices and fuel scarcity threw a pall over the local economy. Vacant lots became gardens and women took over traditionally male jobs, including those of taxi drivers and clerks. The losses, however, were far more than in terms of employment. Lives were lost, and the honor roll erected on the lawn of the courthouse continued to grow.

Shelby County's first World War I casualty was Paul Cross, son of The Reverend Mr. S. J. Cross, minister of the West Street Methodist Church. Ironically, the telegram arrived at the manse on a Sunday. News of other deaths followed, but because of delayed reports, some arrived after the Armistice. In all, around 1,000 county men served in the conflict, and forty-two were listed as dying either in action or due to disease contracted overseas. After the Armistice, life in Shelby County returned to normal, and local workers were able to save money again as prices dropped to their former levels.

In 1920, Reverend and Mrs. S. J. Cross presented the first Paul Cross Medal, a Memorial to their son, Paul, who gave his life while serving in World War I. The award recognized the basketball player who had exhibited outstanding playing ability throughout the season, as well as a good mental attitude toward sports and studies, while maintaining a high level of scholarship.

The year 1920 also began the most prosperous decade in the Shelbyville furniture industry, even though one large entity failed in 1926. The small, central Indiana town boasted the title, " The Little Grand Rapids," due to its high number of furniture manufacturers. Statistically speaking, sixteen was an astounding number of furniture factories for a community Shelbyville's size. The comparison to Michigan's major furniture manufacturing center was not only a source of intense county pride, but also a real boon for the local workforce. Factories employed from thirty-five to over three hundred workers.[11]

Leon Garrett worked at Shelbyville's Spiegel Furniture Factory, founded by Christian Spiegel in 1889. To supplement Leon's income, his wife, Laura, maintained a regular schedule of her own — working as a domestic in a number of local homes.

Shelby County, and Shelbyville, offered residents Midwest living at its best, and provided them with good schools, excellent houses of worship, and a wide range of leisure activities. The annual Shelby County Fair drew thousands of visitors, and traveling stage productions added another dimension to cultural venues. The shows' promoters did not ban Negroes, but they did mandate specific seating arrangements.

Unfortunately, this was also the practice of the local movie houses. There was a section for Negroes in each of the local theatres. Inside, projectors screened the films that Hollywood churned out at breakneck pace during the 1920s and 1930s.

"Talkies" were very popular attractions. Prior to their invention, motion picture fans watched silent movies accompanied by subtitles. Local pianists and organists, such as highly accomplished Shelbyville musician, Katherine "Katie" Hinschlaeger, provided the necessary music for the productions. The local population looked forward to seeing a good movie on the weekend.

Shelbyville business and industry had a long history of offering high paying jobs to workers, regardless of race. Hence, the Negro population held stable jobs. Other towns and cities offered Negroes jobs, but primarily in janitorial or maintenance positions.

Local Negroes held very good jobs, and their wages equaled those of their white neighbors. Many of those jobs were either in the furniture factories or at the prestigious Chambers Range Company, the manufacturer of a kitchen stove whose famous slogan was, "It cooks with the gas turned off!"

Life after World War I lulled Americans into a false sense of security. The change was to come radically, and swiftly, in October of 1929. In one fell swoop, American industry and banking suffered a mighty blow, and it would take years to recover from its effects. The nation began an era known as The Great Depression.

The Garretts, like so many working families, did the best they could after the stock market crashed. When the bottom dropped out of the economy, they had been married only three years. What's more, they were new parents. Day by day, and week by week, they pulled together to get through the hard times, but their plight was in no way unique to the area. In fact, Indiana fared no better than its neighboring states during the height of the financial crisis.

The Depression hit the farm belt very hard. Between 1929 and 1933, farm income dropped by more than half. Yet, even with the sixty-percent drop in farm prices, production fell by only six percent. Individual farmers toiled to produce even more grain, milk, and livestock to offset the lower prices. The surprising result was a surplus. A surplus, however, was not always good news.

Far from a boon, the surplus resulted in stagnation. America could not export the excess because foreign demand was down. To compound matters, a combination of drought and insect infestation, when added to the bank failures, took a high toll on American farmers.

Shelby County farmers suffered mightily in the Depression. Farm after farm went to the auction block for back taxes. In many cases, men left the land their grandfathers had cleared to seek work in towns and cities; but openings were scarce, and the displaced farmers found the job market nearly closed.

Trains continued to ply the tracks between Chicago and Cincinnati, and with them came a a colorful group of men. These so-called "hobos" worked whenever they could find jobs, but, by and large, they depended upon the kindness of families living near the railroad for food. Participating homes were "marked" to avoid an angry confrontation with a homeowner in no mood to share his limited stores.

Among these homes was a small, circa 1869, white clapboard home located at 146 East Broadway, the residence of Lewis and Melinda Schott, the author's grandparents. Only one block from the railroad, it was a typical stop. Occasional, hushed comments and reminiscences of feeding those needy men provided the listeners with the only living testament of their tender charity and compassion.

As the Depression dragged on, it exacted a price from every segment of society, eventually planting a seed of distrust for banking in people across America. Job opportunities were few and far between, so, in the face of flagging infrastructure, the federal government responded with programs of its own — programs designed to employ the hundreds of thousands of unemployed in an effort to further public projects.

Such projects yielded tremendous benefits to communities, large and small. In the midst of such a challenging time, Shelby County families tried their best to reassure their children that a better life was just around the corner. In the end, this type of hope and inspiration helped adults come to grips with day to day struggles.

Despite the hardships of The Great Depression, Leon and Laura Garrett never lost their jobs, and they managed to provide for their growing family. The two of them reared their children with faith in God and sincere determination. Active, devout members of The Second Baptist Church, the Garrett family embraced church activities with enthusiasm.

When the national economy began to rebound, and its factories" tooled up," America's Heartland mended its financial wounds and found the stamina to heal. As prices eased and tensions lessened, Leon and Laura breathed a sigh of relief. The focus and concentration that they placed in faith paid off in dividends for their children. For during the Depression, their family grew by three, with the births of a second son and two daughters, James Edward Garrett (b. February 4, 1931), Mildred Sue Garrett (b. September 14, 1933), and Laura Mae Garrett (b. July 13, 1935).

Leon and Laura joined other church parents to sponsor and

chaperone a wide variety of activities for the congregation's off-spring. The church stressed Bible as a central theme of daily life, and the Garrett household followed that lead.

The family home sat on East Locust Street, among others of the same size and style. Long before the idea of a family room surfaced in architecture, the average American house included basic rooms. These rooms included a kitchen, a dining room, a living room, two or three bedrooms, one bathroom, a front porch, often an enclosed back porch, and a basement with room for a water heater and a furnace. In addition, there was the requisite coal room with a large, rectangular metal door at ceiling level, easily accessible through the outside wall.

If a family included several children, the youngsters shared bedrooms as a matter of pure necessity. Not all home sites included a garage. Those that did exist were small, detached, one-car structures commonly built along the scores of alleys that sliced through nearly every city block. Back yards and side yards sported clotheslines and, occasionally, a shimmering garden ball that caught the afternoon sun. The gleaming, old fashioned, garden ornaments threw slivers of dancing light against the siding and reflected in the windows, much to the delight of adults and children.

The two Garrett brothers shared a bedroom, as did their sisters. The entire family spent evenings together. The children concentrated on homework or enjoyed music and dramatizations broadcast over the tall, floor-model radio in the living room. Both Leon and Laura read, as did their children. Like many of the working families in Shelbyville, their lives revolved around job, school, and church.

Only a few people owned more than one automobile at that time. In contrast to today, if a man owned a pick-up truck for his job, that vehicle served as the sole form of family transportation. When the boys were "kids," as Jim put it, Leon drove a 1935 Pontiac. Family outings were special, and the joy of riding through the countryside was heightened when they could go together as a family. However, weekdays, Laura did most errands on foot, including grocery shopping.

Over forty, small, neighborhood grocers served the town. In addition, several pharmacies delivered needed medications by bicycle messenger. Huge wire baskets bolted to brightly shining handlebars proclaimed the name of the particular dispensary to all onlookers. Cars weren't essential to everyday life, because businesses were scattered throughout the town.

More importantly, after supper walks served couples and families in two ways, as forms of good exercise and as vital social outlets. Typically, seasons and elements permitting, early evening found people sitting outdoors — perfectly positioned on their front porches. There, from a glider, a chair, or a porch swing, they could easily look up from the paper or a magazine and visit with passersby.

Consequently, in the pre-television, pre-air conditioning era, neighbors actually got to know one another. In terms of small town lifestyles, the late 1930s and early 1940s stood out as a gentler, kinder time in which to rear children.

On Saturday night, the downtown area churned with activity. Throngs of people crowded the wide sidewalks around the Public Square and milled along the two main streets leading in and out of it. Conversations hummed above the noise of footfalls and the wheels of prams and strollers as families enjoyed a night "on the town." Several drug stores featured fancy soda fountains, and at least two cafeterias served complete home-cooked meals twice a day.

Few venues offered breakfast. Generally, the Hotel Shelby and one or two smaller area restaurants were the only eateries that served breakfast as a service to the traveling public.

The wide variety of small businesses that lined the streets offered shoppers literally everything, from soup to nuts.

When Jim was asked about going downtown Saturday nights, the query awakened vivid memories of the crowded sidewalks. Saturday nights offered folks a chance to visit with others in a casual, unhurried atmosphere. Store windows were full, and window-shopping was a favorite pastime of old and young. Several sporting goods shops tempted small boys with their wares. Shiny ball mitts and leather basketballs glowed and reflected in the tall, gleaming, storefront windows.

This scene was replicated across the Midwest. It was a time when small town shopping was the centerpiece of retail activity. The Interurban Railway connected Shelbyville with Indianapolis and offered hourly service. The first car left town at 5:30 AM, and the last car pulled out of Indianapolis at 11:30 PM. The last car was usually loaded with late commuters and theatergoers. Freight traffic included stock cars that pulled out of town at 5:00 AM. Neighbors on the north side of town certainly didn't need an alarm clock. The cacophony of mooing, squealing, and snorting made enough noise "to wake the dead."

However useful the rail line was to business and commuters, it was a mode of transportation that served the wider public only as an occasional treat. Those rare trips could have included a visit to the huge Vonnegut Hardware store in downtown Indianapolis or a day at the sweeping Indiana State Fair Grounds. All in all, Shelbyville carried on its business as a very ordinary town within driving distance of the state capital, and its children shared common interests with their counterparts in surrounding counties.

As a youngster, William Garrett was an active boy and enjoyed the company of his younger brother. His sisters, Mildred and Laura, were four and six years younger than

William, who quickly acquired the nickname of "Bill." Although they seldom played with their older brothers, the girls remember vividly how Bill babysat with them when their mother went to work.

Neither of the sisters has a strong recollection of any specific times with their oldest brother, but both women recall that he showed them a great deal of kindness and patience. Laura's one special memory is of Bill playing jacks with her on the front porch. The Garrett parents instilled a good sense of teamwork in their children, so young Bill recognized his responsibilities to his younger siblings, and he took them seriously. He had learned duty and responsibility by example.

Laura Garrett felt very comfortable leaving her older son to oversee his two, active, younger sisters when he was home from school. He was more than able to handle the two little girls, and he knew he could count on close neighbors in case of an actual emergency situation.

Negro children were not permitted to swim at Porter Pool, the local public swimming facility. This recreational roadblock forced Negro parents to teach their children to swim elsewhere. Consequently, summer church outings included picnics along area streams, where children frolicked under the watchful eyes of supervising adults. Among the tributaries available were Big Blue River, Sugar Creek, and Flat Rock River. Second Baptist Church favored an area known as Perry's Bottom, located in the countryside, a little southeast of Shelbyville along a small creek with a swimming hole.

Although the youngsters enjoyed church carry-in dinners, a favorite event was the "Hobo Party." Everything was carefully planned for this pedestrian escapade. Church members chaperoned the children on a designated route. Each child carried a sack on a stick. By the time the little travelers returned to the church, their sacks bulged with snacks accumulated at each home along the way. Treats ranged from fresh pieces of fruit to popcorn.

After a long walk, the children made the most of the contents of their bags. Despite the high popularity of these parties, they held second place to the annual trip to the Cincinnati Zoo. That particular trip was the highlight of the year.

After extensive advance planning with The New York Central Railroad, congregation members squired the children from the church to the local train depot, a small brick building which sat just a few stops down the line from Indianapolis' sprawling Union Station, the very first "Union Station" in the nation.

When questioned, older church members recalled their personal memories of those trips. Excited voices echoed along the platform as anxious youngsters scampered up the metal steps into the train car. Happy faces pressed against the windows and amazed eyes glued on the mammoth carts rolling toward the train. The tall, wood ends rattled on the carts. Heavy, metal wheels clattered across the pavement toward the car behind the coach full of children. Breathless, staccato sentences bounced from seat to seat and from child to child.

The stationmaster stood to one side and proudly orchestrated his crew in the often practiced, well-timed chore of loading the train. The men struggled with heavy, white fabric mailbags and a variety of large boxes. They pulled them from the flat carts and shoved them into the gaping door of the mail car. The easy rhythm of their arms could have been put to music.

Each man worked deftly, as if his every move was ticked off by the second hand of the clock high on the wall inside the depot waiting room. The crew needed to accomplish the mail transfer quickly in order for the train to pull out of the station precisely on schedule. In a matter of seconds, the steam locomotive puffed and lurched into motion from a dead stop. Minutes later, the big engine surged down the rails, bound for points south, including Greensburg and a number of other small towns along the metal ribbon that led toward the Queen City of the Ohio.

The youngsters chatted and giggled as they traveled the eighty or so miles along the "Big Four" toward Ohio, where they disembarked in Cincinnati's Union Station. Once on the platform, the children followed the adults through the huge building and stared up in awe at its tall ceilings. As they walked slowly toward the signature arch of the building's east entry, the small troop glimpsed the crests of the hills that overlooked the city and commanded a fine view of the mighty Ohio River.

Once outside, the group boarded a bus for the Cincinnati Zoo. After a day of animals and snacks, the adults loaded the children into a truck. Today, as adults, the children who made those trips laugh when they recall what fun it was to ride all the way home in the back of an open truck.

Bill's younger brother, Jim, recounts those memories with great joy. Although he deems his youth as far from perfect, he finds great solace in the fact that so many people worked together to make his life happy and secure. He praises the efforts of all those dedicated parents in Shelbyville's Negro community who offered valuable exposure to their growing children.

Leon and Laura Garrett bore witness to a Christian life and a strong work ethic. They encouraged their sons to earn extra money by raking leaves, shoveling snow, and running errands. In addition, both parents stressed the importance of a good education. Negroes attended The Booker T. Washington School through the sixth grade, at which time they enrolled in Shelbyville Jr. - Sr. High School.

Chapter Three

Young Bill Garrett displayed a competitive nature at a very tender age, and he eagerly participated in any and all neighborhood games. Before the age of eight, he demonstrated the serious, internal discipline of a committed athlete — a discipline that hinted at his lifelong pursuit of personal excellence. One example is his entry into a very unusual county contest.

The Works Progress Administration organized community activities nationwide during The Great Depression. Barely two weeks before his tenth birthday, nine-year-old Bill read about a new contest open to boys.

On March 28, 1939, *The Shelbyville Republican* ran a front-page article announcing a countywide marble tournament co-sponsored by the WPA and the newspaper. Over a period of two weeks, each of the eighteen county elementary schools conducted its own, "in-house," marbles contest. The individual winner from each school competed against his peers in the final rounds of the tournament held at Kennedy Park, adjacent to the Shelby County Fairgrounds.

The newspaper used given names for its articles, so when the sports editor listed the finalists, he reported that William Garrett had won the right to represent The Booker T. Washington School. In the final round, ten-year-old William won two straight games in front of a large crowd. He soundly defeated Eldon Hayden, the other semi-finalist, who represented

Cooper Elementary School, located on State Road 44 in Hendricks Township, about half way between Shelbyville and Franklin.

The newspaper featured the results of the County Marbles Tourney on the front page. A large picture of Bill and the runner-up dominated the upper left side on "page one," beneath the banner. Just below the headline proclaiming his victory, Bill flashed his trademark smile, as he proudly clutched the trophy to his chest.

Sport was "king" to growing boys, and participating in sports completely absorbed the "under-twelve set" in the school system. Unlike other Negro elementary schools across Indiana, Booker T. Washington School was not forced to compete against segregated institutions. In contrast, the larger, city school system included Booker T. Washington on par with all the other elementary schools. In light of that fact, it is no surprise that budding athletes, both Negro and white, met each other at an early age.

Bill Garrett and George Glass played basketball against one another in grade school. Bill played for Booker T. Washington School and George played for Charles Major School.

Today, Glass, a retired attorney living in Bloomington, Indiana, proudly touts that his one "claim to fame" is that at one time he was able to guard Bill Garrett. However, he admonishes his audience to view that fact in the proper context.

After all, he and Bill were only in the fifth grade at the time. As they matured, the two boys went their separate ways, at least in terms of their primary interests. Soon, Bill and some of the other boys towered in height over George. For that reason alone, it didn't take long for George to decide that, in the long run, the classroom held much more promise for him than the gymnasium.

In stark contrast to many of his classmates, Bill's athletic prowess drew the attention of onlookers very early. Even during grade school, coaches, parents, and players recognized him as a standout basketball player. Along with teammates Marshall Murray and Emerson Johnson, Bill developed his basic skills under the able tutelage of the venerable Dr. Walter Fort, the head of Booker T. Washington School.

Walter Stanton Fort was born in Fort Royal, Tennessee, in 1888. In many ways, the name of his birthplace forecast his future. As an adult, Fort carried himself with an innate sense of self, proud to be one of the first generation of free-born Negroes who were the children of former slaves. His parents, Forest and Lucy Fort, moved to Evansville, Indiana, about 1900. Known as a child "prodigy" at an early age, Fort read unceasingly.

Fort worked hard in school. He attended two institutions of higher learning, Butler University and Indiana University, before he earned a Bachelor's Degree in Education from Indiana State Teachers College in 1908, at the age of twenty. That same year, he left Evansville and traveled to Webster County, Kentucky, where he taught school and married one Anna P. Ashby. Although they had no children of their own, Walter and Anna adopted and reared a son, Charles Morgan. A few years — and a few promotions later — Fort took a job as principal in the Boonville, Indiana, grade school.

The Superintendent of Schools, W. F. Vogel, later moved to Shelbyville and urged his former teacher to come to serve as both teacher and principal at Booker T. Washington. For 22 years, Fort taught grades four through six on the second floor of Booker T. Washington School.[12] Catherine Starky taught grades one through three on the first floor. Fort's involvement in grades four through six positioned him perfectly to become personally involved in elementary school athletics. Thus, Fort added a third hat.

An avid supporter of every child in his care, the multi-talented Fort took on the job of athletic director and coach. Unlike his local contemporaries, Dr. Fort attended every function involving his students. No youngster under his guidance could have had a finer, more dedicated leader. Yet Fort's influence reached far beyond the confines of Booker T. Washington School.

In a wider community role, he supervised and administered a highly respected competition for excellence in handwriting, a competition open to all local elementary school students. Participation was nearly total among all the grade schools.

Every enterprising, Shelbyville grade school student worked hard to earn one of those writing certificate. This author was among those who practiced handwriting and aspired to bring home the highly desired prize.

Dr. Fort signed every elegant parchment certificate in graceful calligraphy. Each winner treasured the award bearing the name of the prestigious, gentleman educator. His flowing script was unmistakable, and the care with which he signed each award only emphasized the importance he placed on good penmanship. Thanks to Walter Fort and the students at Booker T. Washington School, Shelbyville maintained racial harmony long before any of its neighboring Central Indiana communities.

George Glass remembers Fort this way, "Dr. Walter Fort was a very distinguished gentleman of the highest caliber. I credit him with promoting the sense of decency and honor evident between Shelbyville's Negro and white citizens."

Booker T. Washington School students attributed their educational success to the mentoring of Dr. Fort and his staff. Teachers instilled a strong foundation in their students — a foundation based on the old-fashioned work ethic, dogged determination, pride in individual accomplishment, and personal self-esteem. Taken in sum, their combined efforts prepared students to move into the integrated junior and senior high school system with no fear of failing to conform socially or failing to perform academically.

Grade school years make an indelible impression on children. Put simply, some memories never fade. Don Robinson was in the fifth grade at Thomas A. Hendricks School when he first he played against Bill Garrett in the city grade school championship tournament. Even as a fifth grader, Bill amazed onlookers with his talent, and their comments weren't lost on young Don.

"All the parents talked about it. All the players talked about it. We all knew he was going to be *good*, but we didn't realize just *how* good!"

Chapter Four

On Sunday morning, December 7, 1941, near the end of the first semester of Bill's sixth grade year, the Empire of Japan attacked US Naval forces stationed at Pearl Harbor, Hawaii. America was at war. Before that time, US armed forces made preparations, but held out hope that the nation could avoid fighting in another overseas war. In 1940, the federal government instituted the draft. Conscription offices issued the first call for men in June of 1941. Until that time, the only Shelby County involvement was the seemingly routine mobilization of the local National Guard unit to Camp Shelby, Mississippi in August of 1941.

The first report of "Pearl" was firmly embedded in the mind of everyone who heard it. Man or woman, adult or child — to a person — each would recall for his or her lifetime the precise circumstances under which the news came.

City fathers mandated black out ordinances, and the Garrett household joined their neighbors all across the city. Every evening, heavy coverings hung over all windows after dusk. Even though the actual fighting took place thousands of miles away, a raid surprised the city one night in the late fall.

In November of 1943, an invading force from Camp Atterbury, a training and deployment installation located in adjacent Johnson County, attacked Shelbyville. However, the incoming soldiers had no idea that a defense company waited for them. Some practice shooting occurred, a few tanks rolled through the streets, and top city officials were captured. Just who won was not clear, but the entire incident was over quickly, and, for the most part, few citizens even knew it had happened.[13]

Shortages and rationing brought back memories of the dreaded Depression. New cars were not available, so bicycles experienced a virtual rebirth as a popular mode of transportation. Food supplies became more and more limited, as did public services. For example, after April of 1943, no private phones could be installed. Even the morning toast suffered when jams and jellies were placed off limits in October. Tax rates fell, but only because of a money surplus unable to be spent.

Ironically, the first casualty of World War II, Gerald Owen Smith, held the surname of the first county casualty of the Civil War. Smith, head storekeeper on the U.S.S. Tennessee, died at Pearl Harbor.

Local losses escalated, and a number of local "boys" died on D-Day when Allied forces landed on the beaches of Normandy. Among those was Cecil Lanning. In all, Shelby County listed fifty-six casualties.

Parents tried to shield their children from war news, but many little boys found it exciting. Across the county, mothers ran their households while their husbands fought overseas. It was a difficult time for families, therefore, the entire county community pulled together to help those in need, especially recently widowed women with children and orphans. Many male teachers were drafted or enlisted; and, as a result, staffing was sorely strained, both at the elementary and the secondary levels.

In 1942, there were no signs of an early cessation of hostilities, and children, burdened by the very uncertainty of their future, tried to concentrate on their schoolwork. It was under these circumstances that Bill moved into the Shelbyville public school system. There, he joined his white peers and began what would be an exciting, albeit challenging, period of his life.

Bill's seventh and eighth grade experiences further polished his basketball skills. His abilities progressed at a whirlwind pace. By the time he entered the ninth grade, Bill demonstrated great talent on the basketball court, but he had no conception of what lay ahead of him. In fact, as an incoming freshman, he stood on the brink of a tremendous high school athletic experience — an experience that would catapult him to an outstanding professional career.

Bill earned excellent grades in school, so signing up for a number of the school's extra-curricular activities posed no problems for him academically. A committed athlete, he jumped headlong into four sports, although he dropped one of them after his sophomore year. His three varsity sports were track, baseball, and basketball, a trio of sports he played all four years of high school.

He played football for two years, but he decided to drop it and concentrate on the three remaining sports. In the end, he juggled three varsity sports and class work admirably. Most high school freshmen never played with the "big team," yet, according to classmate Glass, Bill played as a sub on the varsity basketball team during his freshman year. His sophomore year, he quickly earned a spot in "the starting five," where he remained a key player for the rest of his high school career.

In 1944, Bill's freshman year, the war was moving toward a conclusion as he and his fellow junior varsity teammates sat on the sidelines at a home basketball game. That night, Bill and his friends watched a skinny sophomore from Anderson, named Johnny Wilson, steal the ball at mid-court and drive to the basket for what everyone thought would be "an easy lay-up."

Instead, what the Shelbyville crowd saw was a totally unexpected feat. Wilson's shot soared above the rim for the first "slam dunk" anyone had ever witnessed. That single shot made an impression on every player who saw it.

During the 1945 season, Bill tried a "dunk." In his attempt, he pinned the ball against the rim and sprained his back. Coach Barnes reacted firmly in the aftermath. He firmly ordered Bill never "to try that again." Week by week that season, the entire team saw Bill grow bigger and stronger. None of them ever questioned his obedience to the coach. They practiced with Bill every day, and, in keeping with Frank Barnes' directive, not one of them ever saw Bill try to do a dunk again.

In addition to basketball, Bill rapidly earned quite a reputation as a runner. All during high school, he won many awards in track and field. Track teammates yearned to do as well as Bill did with noticeably little practice. Don Robinson, Bill's classmate, ran high school track with Bill.

In Don's words, "Bill came out after school, sat up his own hurdles, practiced for about fifteen minutes, ran a couple of laps, grabbed his ball glove, and headed across the street to the baseball diamond. I worked my tail off along with the rest of the guys, and none of us could ever measure up to his performance. Bill's smoothness as a runner made a deep impression on all of us who watched him.

"The coach could always count on Bill to take up the slack when things went badly during a meet. For example, in one particular South Central Conference Meet, the final event was the half-mile relay in which each of the four runners ran one 220-yard leg. The first runner, Bob Stites, handed off the baton to Sammy Sater. Unfortunately, Sammy dropped the baton. By the time Sammy picked it back up, ran as fast as he could, and handed the baton to Bill, the Bears were dead last. In the next 220 yards, Bill passed all seven of the other runners and gave teammate Bill Breck the lead in the final leg. End result? The Bears won."

Bill ran both the high and low hurdles on the track. As a junior, he took first place in the conference in 1946. In addition, he also earned honors as team "high point man" with 50 and 3/4 points.

Fellow teammate, Ray Ewick, who now lives in Visalia, California, noted Bill's exceptional grace on the track. In his words, "I was a sophomore Bill's senior year. At that time, sophomores didn't rate too high in the food chain for high school seniors. I was a good miler and half-miler. Bill congratulated me a couple of times on my performance during the track meets in which we both participated. Since he was such a star, his commendation was a thrill for me.

"I wanted to be like him. He got better and better with every meet. Bill made hurdling look easy, although coupling a steady run with a smooth transitional stride over each hurdle is far from easy. He possessed surprising ability. He was soft spoken and never aggressive."

A superb athlete, in addition to his excellent performances on the track and basketball court, Bill played a "mean" third base on the high school baseball team. However, basketball remained his first love, and he mastered every nuance of the game. Given his talent and performance on the court, it came as no surprise to local fans when, as a junior, he won The 1946 Paul Cross Award, the highest individual basketball award given by the school.

A naturally shy young man, Bill's personality completely transformed his moment he donned a uniform, no matter the sport. Yet, to his most zealous fans, the true transformation took place in the gym. To them, he changed the instant he stepped onto the basketball court with a ball in his hands.

He never wavered in his calm before the packed crowds that filled all 2,200 seats in the Paul Cross Gymnasium. Crowds and pressure never fazed him. Noise didn't bother him at all. Instead, in the midst of pure emotional chaos, he played flawlessly. In fact, to all outward appearances, Bill seemed totally unaware of the crowd. Instead, he focused solely on the court, his teammates, and his opponents' movements. To those who knew the Garrett family well, his demeanor and aplomb were purely genetic.

Not only did the students at Shelbyville High School love Bill Garrett, they simply adored his mother. Quoting Glass, "Laura Garrett was an extremely refined woman with impeccable manners. She carried herself with an easy elegance, and showed her love for her son unashamedly as she watched him perform."

Leon, however, presented a far different picture. According to Glass, Leon Garrett was an extremely quiet man, in stark contrast to his affable wife who openly, and easily, exuded her lively personality. George described Laura as the real "spark" in the Garrett household. Active in community affairs, she often gave programs on Negro history. *The Shelbyville Republican* cited several such appearances by the highly respected and articulate woman.

In spite of their different personalities, Leon and Laura viewed parenting as a team effort, and, together, they instilled high values in their children. To many observers, Laura imparted the pure joy of living in her every movement. Those closest to the family claimed that Bill took after his mother, especially in terms of appearance and manner. His grace on the track impressed those who watched him, and many of his fans pronounced his mesmerizing talent as innate.

His personal attitude was noticeable during any sporting event, but especially in a fiercely contested basketball game. George Glass stated it well. "The closer the score and the bigger the game, the cooler Bill was."

When World War II ended, America began to rebuild her families, her factories, and her morale. Business spurted wildly, and home construction pumped a great deal of money into local economies nationwide. Returning veterans yearned to work hard all week and then pack up the family to attend the high school basketball games on Friday or Saturday night. The Paul Cross Gym earned its reputation as "the place to be" between November and March. In addition to the camaraderie of visiting with old friends, the newly discharged GIs had their first look at a new player — a player who would capture the hearts of all the local fans.

The 1945-46 season was far from a disappointment, especially in terms of excitement for the home crowd. Game after game, the fans roared wildly, as the gangly junior center moved with the agility of a dancer and the strength and grace typical of a naturally gifted athlete.

As the pivot man on the varsity basketball team, Bill averaged 12.4 points per game. Critics and sportswriters consistently rated him one of the best centers in Indiana high school basketball. Paul Cross Award Committee members lauded him as "a fine sportsman, a fine athlete, and a good student." (*Squib*, 1946).

At the end of the 1946 season, the loss to rival Columbus in the Sectional disappointed the Bears' fans. Bill fouled out near the end of the game, and the team, as a whole, vowed that they would do better in '47. In response, Coach Barnes brought all his varsity players out early in the spring, immediately after the end of the tournament season. He was convinced that running brought rewards in terms of lean, strong players.

After one particular spring practice, Don Robinson offered Bill a ride home on his sleek Cushman motor scooter. When Coach Barnes looked out the door of the gym and saw the two boys climbing aboard, he came running.

Don claims he can still hear Coach Barnes' voice booming across the parking lot. "Robinson, if he doesn't get home in one piece, you are in *big* trouble."

Those words had clout. Don froze, waited a few seconds, and then rode away very carefully. One thing was certain, Don wasn't about to incur the coach's wrath by hurting the star player on the basketball team. Was Bill smiling as he rode behind his friend as they "putzed" down 2nd Street toward Jefferson Avenue?

No account confirms or denies it, but Bill's keen sense of humor supports the affirmative. In any case, Don reports that they both arrived home safely and spent the rest of the summer getting ready for their senior year on the team.

Encouraged by their success in the previous year, all the players looked forward to the upcoming season. They expected a good year, but they had no clue to what events lay ahead of them. Unbeknownst to them, their next eleven games would not only set the stage for a spectacular end to Bill's four-year career at Shelbyville High School, but they would also enshrine the 1947 Shelbyville Golden Bears into a very exclusive club.

Chapter Five

In order to understand the relationship among the players on the 1947 Shelbyville Golden Bears basketball team, one needs to heed the words of team member, Bill Breck.

"In thinking about Bill Garrett and his impact or influence on his teammates, I first need to explain my perception of the '47 team. We lived in a different era. Team members didn't show their emotions with 'high fives' or individual theatrics to draw attention to themselves as the result of good plays, nor did they show signs of temper when things went poorly. Coaches were in total control and would not tolerate such behavior. Likewise, young men and women of that period were instilled with a sense of pride and responsibility. Parents were supportive of coaches, administrators, and teachers. With this background, I turn to Bill Garrett and his influence.

"Bill led by example, not by talk. He was a quiet, reserved young man —mannerly and always well behaved. He was friendly, cheerful, and highly respected by all. Even those who knew him only as fans watching him on the basketball floor were greatly impressed with his athletic ability and demeanor. I do not recall even one time ever hearing or reading a critical word about Bill. Bill's quiet, confident manner, along with his superior athletic skills, drew people of all ages to him. At school, or on the basketball floor, Bill was all business. He had a strong, competitive drive. He would not let opponents rattle him. This transferred to the team. Bill, with all of his basketball success, was still just plain Bill Garrett. He never was bigger than the team."

Another teammate, Loren "Hank" Hemingway, puts it this way. "I remember Bill mainly as a quiet, unassuming person. A strong competitor, Bill was always quick to give credit to his teammates for a win and equally as quick to take the blame for a loss. I remember his mother, and I knew her as a very kind and caring person — traits that also applied to Bill. Her Kool-Aid and cookies were always a great treat to those of us who went to her kitchen after a game of basketball behind the Booker T. Washington School.

"Perhaps my most important memory is the first time I met Bill. It was in the fall of 1943, after the school year had started. My family moved from Franklin to Shelbyville, and it was really a 'down time' for me. Within a short time after our move, high school basketball tryouts were held for the freshman team. As I walked onto the floor of the old Paul Cross Gym, the first person to say anything to me was Bill. He looked up and said, 'Hey, man, do you want to shoot with me?' The move from Franklin was forgotten in an instant."

Among the team members interviewed for this book, one common thread weaves the young men together as a unit. That thread is Bill Garrett. One cannot overestimate his importance to the 1947 team, yet, considering all the first person assessments of his personality, he would be the last one to agree on that point. On the firm foundation of purpose and persistence, Coaches Frank Barnes and Arthur "Doc" Barnett began the 1946-47 season with a sense of anticipation neither man had felt before.

The local newspaper heralded the team as "promising," and Sports Editor Bill Holtel wrote more than one column in praise of both the team and the coaching staff. As the season began, the atmosphere at home games was nearly electric. Everyone in the stands, from the concessionaires to the fans, seemed to sense the importance of each home contest.

Even more excited were those people who took the time to follow the team on the road for all the away games. In addition to the players' parents, scores of season ticket holders drove mile after mile to watch the Bears play that season. There were no interstate highways, and Indiana weather could be brutal during the basketball season; but, in spite of inclement weather and treacherous, two-lane roads, the diehard fans who took to the highways on the trail of '47 did not come away disappointed.

Citing the 1947 *Squib*, "the 1946-47 season boded well for the Shelbyville Golden Bears. Five returning seniors made up the starting five. The Bears not only had the experience, height, fight, and spirit, but they also possessed that all-important desire to win."

A press report stated the following, "The forwards were big 'Hank' Hemingway, the boy who did a big job of rebounding all season. Hank really helped Garrett under the basket and aided Marshall 'Speed' Murray, the one-handed specialist on the squad who was a valuable man with his height. At center was the one and only, all-state, 'bouncing' Bill Garrett, who did everything possible all the time. He led the team in scoring and played nice defensive ball, too.

"At the guard positions were the 'little boys' of the team, Emerson Johnson and Bill Breck. Everyone knew that when 'Emmie' got a hold on the ball, it was almost a sure two points. He was a 'dead eye' from the field, and also gained all-state recognition."

Never one to exhibit any kind of emotion, Emerson's facial expression remained sober. His stoic nature on the court was the source of great comment among fans in the stands.

Bill Breck, on the other hand, was the "ball hawk" on the team. Always in everyone's hair, it made no difference to Bill whether "his man" was big or little, he still "took" him. Bill was a hard driver — always talking and keeping up team spirit. His fervor against larger opponents instilled a high level of respect from both benches.

The reserves were all juniors. Of these, Don Chambers and Everett Burwell saw the most action. These boys were good reserves, and Coach Barnes never hesitated to call on them. Bill Breedlove also saw considerable action during the season. The remaining players were Walt Wintin, Don Robinson, John Simpson, and Louis Bower.

Press clippings from both *The Shelbyville Democrat* and *The Indianapolis Star* provide rich details for the 1946-47 Golden Bears' Season. Long lines formed early for season tickets, and judging from the amount of time required to buy tickets, fans had high hopes for the local team. Student enthusiasm ran high, and that youthful fervor only echoed the emotional atmosphere of the town as a whole. Football season seemed to drag for those hoop fanatics who looked forward to the opening game of the basketball season.

From the earliest days of the season, Central Indiana coaches spotted a rare combination of talent and teamwork in the Golden Bears. The opening game saw Franklin bow to the Bears 37-27. Then, Seymour lagged behind at the closing buzzer 46-30. Connersville lost a rout to the Bruins 56-29. Even mighty Muncie Central suffered an eleven point loss, 46-35. Two losses followed quickly. First, Lafayette "Jeff" edged out Shelby's five 41-39 and then Columbus' Bulldogs piled on 9 points at the end of the game to beat the Bears 42-33. However, it didn't take long for the hometown boys to be on the winning end again. Next, the Bears beat Greensburg

47-30. An eight-point loss to Indianapolis Shortridge fueled the team's need for another Conference win, and Franklin couldn't get past the Bears in a second try. They lost to Coach Barnes' quintet 38-35.

Greensburg tried again, too, but they lost by even more than they had the first time they played the Bears, going down by 21 points, 39-18.

Returning to the 1946-47 *Squib* commentary, after a fast start to the season, "The Bears improved steadily, and by February, they were definitely the 'dark horse' of the tourney. No one gave them much credit during the season, but Coach Frank Barnes and Assistant Arthur 'Doc' Barnett knew that this was Shelby's year. All season long, the fans were thrilled by the brilliant offensive and defensive work of the team."

In the third game after the Holiday Tourney, Shelbyville hosted the undefeated Terre Haute Garfield Purple Eagles, a team that had its eyes set on a perfect season! Coach Willard Kehrt was bringing his team back to his hometown gymnasium for a "battle royal." The Shelbyville crowd was primed for the contest, and Coach Barnes had prepared his young men for a fierce game. That it was.

Officiating that night, Indianapolis brothers John and Earl Townsend had their hands full. At the half-time break, the two referees approached Nate Kaufman, a fellow official who lived in Shelbyville. Because of the tense atmosphere in the gym and the high emotion among the fans, the two brothers were concerned for their personal safety once the final horn had sounded. Kaufman contacted the Indiana State Police, and, after the game, uniformed troopers quickly moved the men out of town with a full police escort. Among the twenty regular season games, home or away, that 52-44 Garfield loss to Shelbyville was the only game in which IHSAA officials asked for protection for any contest involving Frank Barnes' team.[14]

In the final regular season game, the Golden Bears inflicted a 16-point defeat on Connersville with a score of 49-33. Going into the Sectionals, the Bears had a record of eight and three, with a total of 453 team points — a season average of 41.18 points per game. Because hopes ran high for a win in the first round of the State Tournament, fans were nervous, and tickets were definitely "the hot commodity."

The scores, no matter how impressive, fail to describe the actual experiences of the team members during their high school basketball careers — especially those experiences "on the road." Segregation was alive and well throughout Indiana, and the young players who traveled to "away games" saw a world far less kind and receptive. Team members recall vividly when a restaurant refused to serve the team because of the inter-racial mix of the players.

Coaches Barnett and Barnes had a standard reply to such overtures. In one player's words, Coach Barnes would simply look the owner right in the eye and say very calmly, "If you won't serve those boys, you won't serve any of us."

For the most part, that ended the controversy. In those instances when the owner steadfastly refused to serve the Negro players, Coach Barnes simply ushered the team outside and took them to another establishment.

Even more disgusting was the verbal abuse hurled at the players at the away games. Most disturbing was the fact that the verbal abuse not only came from the fans in the stands, but also from coaches on the host schools' benches. These incidents of discrimination were not isolated cases by any stretch of the imagination. Officials ignored them — acting as if they had never happened. The society of the time took no responsible action to thwart cruelty, even when it was aimed at teenagers.

Today, when such behavior would be tantamount to professional suicide in coaching, the situation seen in 1947 is unfathomable. Looking back, it is hard to imagine what Bill, Emerson, and Marshall underwent while they played for Shelbyville.

If Conference play were not enough of a racial insult, consider what happened during Tournament play. Those contests heaped even more insults on the Negro players. Tournaments often comprised teams Shelbyville did not play during the regular season, and the three Negro players on the Bears were constant victims of racially pointed remarks from their opponents.

Although nothing was done at the administrative level to stop these incidents, the Golden Bear trio knew they could count on their coaches for moral support. There was absolutely no hint of discrimination either among the players or between the coaches and the players on the Shelbyville team. Both Barnett and Barnes stood tall, not only as outstanding men among their coaching peers, but also as excellent role models for their young high school players.

Teams traveled by bus, at that time, and players routinely helped one another with homework and test preparation on road trips. Those student-athletes who were extremely good in science and math helped those who needed extra assistance. Over time, what began as strictly athletic relationships, cemented into great friendships. According to one team member, the Bears' deep camaraderie "instilled patience and a deep respect for others that lasted a lifetime."

Walter Wintin appreciated Bill's attitude toward the newer players on the team. A "bench player," Wintin remembered how Bill treated him. "I was the eleventh man on the team — the bottom of the totem pole. He treated me as if I was just as important as the starters. I felt very fortunate to have his friendship."

Chapter Six

The 1947 Sectional Tournament, held on the Bears' home court, proved to be the first in a string of wins that propelled Frank Barnes' players one step closer to their dream: The State Championship.

For the first time since 1944, Shelbyville won its home sectional. That sectional win, in the earliest stage of the tournament, gave Golden Bears fans a hint of the depth possessed by "their team." As *The Shelbyville Democrat* put it, "An avalanche of baskets early in each game enabled the team to coast home in the second half. Both Franklin Township and Columbus fell victim to the scrappy Bears."

The team worked hard in practice the next week, anticipating a rough series in the Greensburg Regional the next weekend. The four teams berthed at Greensburg were Franklin, Madison, North Vernon, and Shelbyville. The Bears drew the 1:15 tip-off against Ray Eddy's Madison Cubs, while Franklin followed in the 2:30 game with North Vernon.

Ticket availability posed severe problems to school authorities. J.W.O. Breck, Superintendent of Schools, anticipated that Greensburg would issue 700 tickets to Shelbyville, but students got "first dibs" on them. The Greensburg gym held 3,160 seats, and the host school received ten percent of that number, or 316. Officials issued twelve complimentary tickets to each of the competing schools for team members, for a total of 48. Only 36 tickets were ordered on this basis, leaving the remaining 2,364 tickets to be divided in two ways: one half equally among the four participating schools, and one-half prorated on enrollment.

Shelbyville's enrollment stood at 555, Franklin's at 381, Madison's at 316, and North Vernon's at 254. Tickets cost $1.60 each and were available with certain caveats. Tickets were to be sold by mail order solely to adults and elementary school students who held season tickets. School authorities required that every ordered ticket be accompanied by an original season ticket. Lost season tickets were honored if specific seat locations were included in the letter requesting tickets, so long as the locations and the names of the holders corresponded with athletic department records.

In the wake of the five seniors' play in the sectional battle, Bears fans eagerly looked forward to the regional series. Emerson Johnson, Marshall Murray, Bill Garrett, Loren "Hank" Hemingway, and Bill Breck gave consistent, dependable performances the preceding weekend. Going into the regional, the Bears' overall season record was 19 wins in 24 games.

The opening game of the Greensburg Regional pitted the Bears against Madison's Cubs, coached by Ray Eddy. Many Southern Indiana fans considered Eddy a "fiery" personality. However, under the calm direction of Coach Frank Barnes, the Bears were ready. In the words of his teammates, that particular tournament game set Bill apart for his high degree of sportsmanship. In that game, Bill's self control rose to the height of legend. Don Robinson remembers that night well, and his words paint a vivid description of exactly what happened.

"One particular player on Madison's team worked Bill over real good. He pinched Bill, elbowed him, and even grabbed his shirt — all the while uttering nasty racial slurs loud enough to be heard from both benches. The Madison coach didn't intercede. He just sat there and watched.

"Shelbyville players and fans were shocked when the Madison bench did nothing to stop the continuing assaults on the quiet Shelbyville center. Such an embarrassing situation might have crushed a more insecure player, but it didn't shake Bill Garrett one bit. In terms of his performance — and true to every game I saw him play — Bill never responded to the rude, unruly opponent. Instead, Bill's response was one of disciplined, excellent ball handling. Bill ignored the ugly words and physical assaults hurled at him. His reaction to the situation was to score 29 points and, in the process, knock the Madison Cubs completely out of the tournament. Bill's actions spoke volumes."

The late Louis B. Means, University of Nebraska Athletic Director in 1947, was a Shelby County native. During the 1970s, this author had the privilege of discussing high school athletics with him. His comments were sage and pointed.

"High school athletes appear strong and confident to most observers, but in fact, they are merely children in adult bodies. The size and skill of a high school player masks the fact that he is a growing child — a child who must deal with adults in adult situations under extreme degrees of pressure. This is a fact roundly ignored by those in charge of athletic competition at the high school level in America."

With those words in mind, consider the immense juggernaut that faced Bill Garrett each and every time he played a game away from home. His tenacity and composure stand as a benchmark for athletes today.

There was never a doubt that Shelbyville fans supported Bill unequivocally, that the coaching staff stood behind him totally, and that his teammates rallied to his side solidly. Yet, even buoyed by all these positives, Bill faced unending waves of personal insult. In the end, he not only weathered the storm, but he emerged from it without so much as a frown on his face. His true character shone through all his travails. Again, the man within the boy overcame daunting, hurtful obstacles and showed all those who watched him the pinnacle of poise and self-control.

Bill's 29 points against Madison iced the game for the Bears and moved the team another step forward by securing a place in the final contest. When the buzzer sounded at the culmination of the evening game, Shelbyville had crushed North Vernon by a score of 55-23. For the first time since 1935, the Golden Bears joined the "Sweet Sixteen."

Again, nervous fans scrambled for tickets. Several local men traveled as far as north as Elkhart and South Bend. They hoped to parlay friendships and business contacts into valuable pieces of pasteboard that would gain them entry to the games in the semi-final round of the tournament.

Rumors ran wild the week after the Greensburg Regional. Frantic fans openly voiced fear that their Bears would be declared ineligible because two of the team members were eighteen years of age. Thankfully, *The Shelbyville Democrat* dispelled the gathering gloom. The sports editor explained to his readers that the IHSAA age limit for high school players was twenty, not eighteen, as had been claimed. Once more, hopes soared for a higher level of play.

Spirited conversations permeated cafes, diners, factories, offices, grocery stores, haberdasheries, grain elevators, feed stores — and, yes, even churches. Talk centered on the upcoming Semi-State. Fans tried to downplay their air of confidence, but their wide grins belied the feeling that victory was truly in the offing.

Many people in the business community voiced their opinions as the games drew nearer. Charles Sindlinger owned a popular meat market. An avid basketball fan, he had a classic response to his customers who had their doubts. "Victory? I can smell it, and I assure you, I have a well-trained nose!"

Administrators wondered if the 3,500 tickets allotted to Shelbyville would be sufficient. Requests arrived by the hundreds. Pleas flooded any possible venue, including the homes of the local postmaster, the mayor, school administrators, and the coaching staff. Mr. Breck's office staff struggled to sort the piles of letters requesting tickets that arrived in their offices on a daily basis. In addition, a sea of envelopes continued to pile up on the desks in the athletic offices at The Paul Cross Gym.

If someone wanted a ticket, they had no compunction at trying to go "around the barn" to get one. Those in charge knew that actual ticket holders numbered 2,400. However, they expected multiple requests. As they began to go through the mail, school officials counted as many as four to eight tickets requests per season ticket holder.

Over two thousand applications poured into the school superintendent's office for the one hundred tickets available to the general public. These orders were over and above the number of tickets formally earmarked for the standard recipients — team members, coaches, and their families.

In addition, student and adult or child season ticket holders were eligible for tickets to the Semi-State. A heavy burden weighed on both Superintendent Breck and his aide de camp, veteran SHS mathematics teacher, J. M. "Mac" McKeand. Finally, the two men chose an open drawing as the fairest way to solve the thorny dilemma.

When all was said and done, the school awarded the remaining sought-after 100 tickets by a lottery. No doubt, the one hundred persons who heard their names announced when their cards were plucked out "of the squirrel cage" breathed a deep sigh of relief. Alas, those without tickets were left to their own devices, many of which were, to say the least, quite ingenious.

Ticket seekers used every possible ploy. Some even feigned professional privilege in order to secure access to the sold-out series. Authentic press passes were hard to come by, yet enterprising "sports writers" invented themselves over-night, only to be disappointed when tournament officials judged their "credentials" unsubstantiated.

The "buzz" continued unabated during the week after the Greensburg Regional win. Basketball fever not only ran rampant in Shelbyville, but it quickly spread to the outlying areas. Radio rescued all those fans without tickets. Broadcasts brought the excitement of Semi-State play into living rooms across Shelby County, as radio feeds linked the entire state to the action-packed contests.

Fans in homes, firehouses, hospitals, and eateries around the state sat rapt in attention. The live, play-by-play broadcast thrilled avid listeners. For those who were relegated to stay at home or at work, the roar of the crowd in Butler Fieldhouse was the perfect acoustical backdrop for the pinnacle in Hoosier high school basketball competition.

Shelbyville fans attending the 1947 Indiana High School Basketball Semi-State Tournament rode a roller coaster of emotion equal to that of thousands of first-time fans who rooted for eleven of the "Sweet Sixteen" teams. Five teams had previous experience at that level. Those teams were Fort Wayne South, Muncie Burris, Bedford, Evansville Central, and Huntington.

Tournament games were physical gauntlets, yet the 1947 series was far less stressful than its predecessors, especially in terms of the time allotted for playing the entire set of games.

In 1947, several weekends separated the levels of tournament play — a situation far from that in the past.

Organizers held the first Indiana State High School Basketball Championship at Indiana University in Bloomington, on March 10-11, 1911. For the next twenty-five years, the "Sweet Sixteen" teams played the entire tournament on a single weekend. All that changed in 1936. Officials abandoned the condensed format and initiated a new schedule that slated the Semi-State and the State Final contests one full week apart.

Shelbyville entered the 1947 Semi State series as the favorite, but as Bob Stranahan, columnist for *The Indianapolis Times*, wrote, "Hoosier hardwood fans are notoriously and particularly hard on the top dog. To make matters worse…the other three contenders are of the smaller school variety and will have the crowd's sympathy."

Bill Garrett was described as the duplicate of Johnny Wilson, star of the 1946 State Champion Anderson Indians. Coaches judged Bill as exceptionally talented at the pivot and a consistently excellent rebounder. In addition, if Frank Barnes' starting five encountered foul trouble, his bench possessed the talent to step in and do a good job.

The Golden Bears defeated a talented Clinton squad in the afternoon game by a score of 48-39, and went on to take down Lawrenceburg by seven points, 44-37. Jubilation reigned at home, but the scant allotment of 800 tickets put a damper on the community's sense of exhilaration. Most local fans assumed that the further the Bears went in the tournament series, the more tickets they would receive. The revelation that 500 of the 800 available tickets would go to students left a cloud of disappointment hanging over the remaining 1,600 season ticket holders, each of whom wanted entry rights into Butler Fieldhouse for the State Finals the following weekend.

Hetty Gray

The core problem was that the Indiana High School Athletic Association's plan issued every participating school a portion of the total tickets for the final series. In one fell swoop, that governing body dispersed 8,500 of the available 14,800 tickets.

Furthermore, each of the twelve schools that lost in the Semi-State round received one hundred tickets. Dispersing those 1,200 tickets shrunk the available ticket pool even more. When each of the "Final Four" schools received its allotment of 800 tickets, another 3,200 tickets disappeared. Of the remaining tickets, IHSAA earmarked 1,900 of them for basketball officials and other dignitaries.

The result was abject disappointment for uncounted numbers of Shelbyville fans who longed to watch their talented Golden Bears play for the ultimate prize in Indiana high school basketball.

Finalists emerged from Semi-State contests held at four selected Hoosier college sites: Ball State University in Muncie, Butler University in Indianapolis, Indiana University in Bloomington, and Purdue University in West Lafayette. "The Final Four" for 1947 were The Shelbyville Golden Bears, The Marion Giants, The Terre Haute Garfield Eagles, and The East Chicago Washington Senators, an even mix of two small and two large schools. The stage was set. Only one week remained, and that week sparked commentary statewide about the contenders' strengths and weaknesses.

State sportswriters, as well as a good percentage of Hoosier high school coaches, predicted that Terre Haute would play against East Chicago in the final game, but their call was cut short. In spite of all their expertise, not a single sportswriter "got it right." When the afternoon games ended, slack-jawed journalists raced to telephones to get their shocked observations into print.

Why? Goliath had fallen, and a determined David stood ready to take on the giant's replacement. The experts' "call" on the outcome of the afternoon series was short-circuited by a determined Golden Bear team from Shelbyville. The feisty group not only put a crimp in the experts' predictions, but it also exposed one particular senior player to a new, more diverse audience. That player astounded the crowd with his talent, much to the joy of fans and scouts.

The first afternoon game erupted in a fierce contest between Terre Haute and Marion. As the final second ticked off the game clock, Terre Haute came out on top, 59-50. Shelbyville met a talented East Chicago team in the second afternoon game. At the end of the first quarter, the Bears had scored only two field goals. Fans were clearly worried, because the score stood at 17-11 in favor of East Chicago. Enter Emerson Johnson. "Emmie" sparked the squad in the second quarter, and Shelbyville tied the game at 24 at the halftime buzzer.

Defense was a real problem for East Chicago that day, and their coach assigned four of his finest players to guard Bill Garrett. Unfortunately for the Senators, three of their four players fouled out before the end of the game. A power drive in the third quarter piled up a 43-36 margin for the Bears, and East Chicago never threatened a Shelbyville victory after that point. With three minutes on the clock, Breck was sidelined with an ankle injury, and the score was 49-43, Shelbyville. East Chicago's foul trouble did not spread to the Golden Bears. Hemingway did foul out, but he was the sole player who ended the game on the bench. The final score was an impressive 54-46 Shelbyville win over the Senators.[15]

Only a few hours lay between the end of the afternoon game and the tip-off of the Championship game that evening. The coaches concentrated on team rest. When Shelbyville and Terre Haute players stepped onto the floor for the tip-off of the final game, their hometown fans went wild. The air was positively electric, and, after the National Anthem, the crowd settled back in the stands in a state of pure anxiety.

Willard Kehrt, gum-chewing, intense Coach of Garfield watched as Hank Hemingway batted in a rebound to give Shelbyville a 2-0 lead early in the first quarter. Two Garfield free throws evened it up, but then Emerson Johnson hit a long one and Bill Garrett flipped in another to give the Bears a four-point lead.

Johnson and Clyde Lovellette traded shots and Bill Breck made it 12 to 6 in favor of the Bears with three minutes remaining in the quarter. Shelby's scoring ace, Bill Garrett, had two personal fouls. Garrett drew the job of guarding six-foot-nine-inch Lovellette. The two teams traded two pointers, and at the end of the first quarter, Shelbyville led 14-8.

Johnson, Shelby's "clutch man," opened the second period with a field goal, but Bob Skitt countered for Garfield. Lovellette tipped in a rebound, was fouled, and made his free throws. That cut the Bear lead to three, 16-13. But, Breck and Johnson drove under to score again. Garfield couldn't hit and Shelbyville couldn't miss, so the score went to 26-15, Bears. Hemingway was charged with his fourth personal foul with a Shelbyville lead of 29-19 and three minutes to go in the first half. Fouls were hampering both Shelby and Garfield. The scoreboard read Shelbyville 33, Garfield 26 at the half-time buzzer.

Bill Garrett opened the third period with a tip-in, and added a free throw for a 36-26 lead. Lovellette batted in two rebounds, but the Bears kept pace. Just after Lovellette hit a one-hander from the corner, little Emerson Johnson hit his 18th and 19th points. That gave Shelbyville a 10-point margin, 43-33.

Johnson poured in two more fielders, but Garfield cut this

to 49-41. Then, Lovellette and Ronnie Bland connected for Garfield as the quarter ended with the score, Shelbyville 51, Garfield 45.

The fourth quarter saw Bears' Coach Frank Barnes insert Hemingway back into the lineup, but he fouled out a few seconds later. Center Lovellette came back with a free throw and batted in a rebound miss for his 23rd and 24th points. Garfield trailed, 51-48, the closest margin since the first period.

Lovellette got his fourth foul, and, in short order, Garrett picked up his fourth foul and Lovellette made a free throw. The Bears came back on a fast break and scored for a 55-51 lead with less than four minutes to play.

Then, Lovellette fouled out. In those last, frantic four minutes, Shelbyville never was in any real danger, but the Bears were threatened by a dauntless, never-say-die Garfield five. Shelbyville gradually pulled away, however, to become the 1947 State Champs by a 68-58 count. In the final period, the Bears shot an average of .437, hitting 7 of 16 shots, while Garfield hit for .217 on 5 of 23.

After the final game, newspaper accounts claimed that a rare blend of "blood, sweat, and tears" resulted in a well-deserved State Championship title for the 1947 Golden Bears. Statewide, the press proclaimed the ten Shelbyville victories as the stellar culmination of a grueling four weeks of combat against a varied mix of talented opponents. The magnificent level of play exhibited by the underrated Bears humbled two "powerhouses" of high school basketball to earn the highest prize in Indiana's foremost high school sport.

When Captain Bill Garrett stood center court with an IHSAA official shortly after the final game on March 22, 1947, in Butler Fieldhouse, thousands of cheering fans fell hushed. Fans and opposing players watched quietly as the graceful Shelbyville senior stood at center court and proudly accepted the trophy on behalf of his coach, his teammates, and his school.

UPI reported that entire teams, as well as individual players, broke eleven state records during the Final Four in 1947. Shelbyville center, Bill Garrett, scored a blistering 91 points over the four game series, surpassing the individual scoring record. Bill's 91 bettered by six points the previous record held by Johnny Wilson, of the 1946 State Champion Anderson Indians and Indiana's 1946 "Mr. Basketball." As a team, the Golden Bears scored 30 field goals in the final game, and the two-team total of 126 points amounted to a consistent barrage of four points per minute.

Shelbyville's 54 free throws eclipsed the record in that department, as did the final score of 68 — an all-time high for an Indiana High School Championship final game. In addition, the Bruins broke the record of most points scored by an opponent in a final series with a total of 180, besting Anderson's total of 160 in 1946. Amazingly enough, the record for most personal fouls also went to The Golden Bears. Even with twenty personal fouls on the scorecard, the Bears emerged victorious.

Three tourney records fell during the 1947 State Finals game. The record for the most individual field goals in a final game went to Shelbyville's Emerson Johnson, a mark that equaled Johnny Wilson's record set in 1946. The Bruins, as a team, tied Anderson's 1946 record of most field goals in the "Sweet Sixteen," with 80 points. The record for the most field goals by any two of the four finalists went to Shelbyville and Terre Haute, with 49. This record tied the record of Anderson and Fort Wayne Central in their 1946 final game.[16]

Bill Garrett's performance in the Final Four heightened the growing interest among out-of-state college basketball scouts. Their interest, however, didn't go unnoticed within Indiana high school basketball's inner circles. Among the most serious "movers and shakers" intimately allied with Indiana high school basketball were officials and fans alike. These groups shared a growing, sincere concern about Indiana's failure to retain its best players for colleges within its borders.

During the 1940s, many of the best Indiana high school players went out of state to play college basketball. Their exodus inspired a high degree of angst for tried and true basketball officials. Consequently, the 1947 State Final Tournament lit a fire under influential men within the highest ranks of Indiana high school basketball.

At first, the fire simply smoldered; but, over time, it flashed into a flame — a flame that exploded into a groundbreaking change in the annals of collegiate basketball. The singular spark for this fire came in the person of a tall, shy, high school center…a player of extraordinary ability…a teenager with the disposition of a seasoned adult…a youngster who was the pride of his small home town …. That player was William Leon "Bill" Garrett, SHS Class of 1947.

Chapter Seven

Calm spread through the Shelbyville dressing room after the final game, and quietly gathered around their coach, Garfield's team reacted in much the same way. Garfield Coach, Willard Kehrt — ironically, a Shelbyville native — thoughtfully commented to the press about the final game.

"Everything went right for them (Shelbyville) tonight. We came out after them, just as they started hitting. We've lost before, just not this season."

In contrast, the scene in the East Chicago Washington Senators' locker room was bleak. Reluctant tears flowed among the downcast players, but center, Ray Ragelis, took the loss the hardest of all. He sat in front of his locker for a long time, his head bowed in grief. Earlier, on the court, he was the first man to step forward and congratulate the Bears on their victory. His congratulations were sincere, despite the fact that, going into the game, he had every reason to believe that his team would win. [17]

Crestfallen and quiet, the Marion Giants filed to their seats during halftime of the second game. In truth, those "in the know" claimed that the squad accepted their defeat as inevitable. Garfield Coach Kehrt looked up into the stands as the players moved to their seats. He spotted Marion Ace Dick Weagley. Kehrt nodded to the teenager and quipped, "Boy, you're a good ball player."

Sportsmanship dominated on every side. Those were the days of decorum and honor. Coaches didn't show extremes of temper or aggravation. Technical fouls were rare. Teachers and coaches commanded respect as much for their personal qualities as for their positions of authority.

Guidance and example prepared young men involved in high school sports to accept victory with humility and to view defeat with objectivity, devoid of shame. One parent of that generation explained the atmosphere of high school sports this way:

"In the end, it was just a game, and in a game — just as in life — things don't always go the way you wish."

At the same time that three disappointed teams, coaches, and carloads of emotionally exhausted supporters left Indianapolis and motored toward their homes, elated Shelbyville fans organized the first of several hometown victory celebrations.

Minutes after Coaches Barnes and Barnett huddled with their players in the locker room of Butler Fieldhouse, they piled into waiting cars for the trip home. An entourage of Indiana State Police cars waited outside the arena. Red lights flashed brightly as the ensemble pulled away from Butler Fieldhouse and made its way out of the state capital.

A little past midnight, the cavalcade rolled to a stop at the bridge across Big Blue River. A shiny fire truck blocked the span at the intersection of Michigan Road and State Road 9. Surprised and excited, Bears players, managers, and coaches scrambled atop the spotless Ariens Fox Pumper.

A shrill mix of sirens cut through the night air as the fire truck and the accompanying police cars slowly glided between the darkened bathhouse of the public pool and the tall grain elevator directly across the street. Exuberant teenagers stared down from the fire truck at the gathering crowd of people along the main thoroughfare.

The fire truck moved at a crawl as it passed before the few remaining downtown homes, two small service garages, the local bus station, and a bevy of small businesses leading to the center of town. Bordering sidewalks teemed with fans, waving wildly to the victorious Golden Bear team.

Five blocks south, the brass-trimmed monster inched its way slowly around the wide ribbon of pavement that circled the business hub of the town, known commonly as "The Public Square." Once it reached the southwest quadrant and rounded The Shelby National Bank on the corner, the pumper turned south onto Harrison Street and crossed the wide intersection at Broadway.

The parade halted before The Shelby County Courthouse that sat just two blocks further south. An impressive stone facility built by the WPA during the Great Depression, the Court House was the focal point for the initial hometown celebration. City officials deliberately chose the location, because they feared that frenzied fans might set random bonfires all around the city.

A roaring blaze greeted an overflow crowd of happy basketball fans. Mayor James Pierce stepped forward and formally welcomed the fire truck and its passengers. Each team member stepped from the vehicle to wild cheers from the fans. School officials cancelled classes the next day, in honor of the team.

Bear supporters jammed around the team and coaches. Raspy voices were a badge of honor. Emotions soared, as people of all ages gave in to the euphoria unique to what became more commonly known in later years as "Hoosier Hysteria." [18]

Newspaper accounts claimed that the celebration equaled,

or surpassed, the observances of the end of World War II. Quoting the local paper, "a howling mob of title-mad basketball fans grabbed the city of Shelbyville by the nape of the neck Saturday night and shook the staid little community until its teeth rattled into the late morning hours of Sunday morning."[19]

The scene in the streets that night was merely a preview of a series of celebrations held for full two weeks after the local team won the state title. Downtown stores plunged into the fray with great enthusiasm. Most of the retailers decorated their windows to coincide with the citywide celebration. The downtown J. C. Penney store offered shoppers a unique display. Window dressers constructed a miniature basketball court featuring teddy bears in gold satin uniforms. All ten bears crowded around a net at end of the court, as Number 9 (Bill Garrett) stood at the top of a ladder and cut down the net.

A Panda bear stood on the sidelines wearing a gray sweater. That particular portion of the diorama delighted dyed-in-the-wool Shelbyville fans. They smiled when they saw that familiar gray sweater — immediately recognizing it as Coach Barnes' game uniform of choice.

For over two weeks, Shelbyville spread out its red carpet. Dignitaries spoke before the team and coaches. Among the most well-known personalities were former Shelbyville native Wilbur Shaw, President of the Indianapolis Motor Speedway and three-time winner of the Indianapolis 500 automobile race. Hollywood contributed Marjorie Main (formerly Marjorie Tomlinson of Fairland, Indiana). A true Hoosier basketball fan, Miss Main broke away from a nationwide tour promoting her new movie, *The Egg and I,* to participate in honoring the champions from her home county.

Accolades came from virtually every quarter. Perhaps the

most amusing to the sportswriters was one, lone fact. Ironically, of all the pundits who predicted the winner of the 1947 state final game, the only man to "get it right" was INS Bureau Editor, Jack Estell — a Shelbyville native.

Estell made his astonishing prediction on February 25, the day before sectional competitions began. At that time, 781 teams were eligible for the crown. Given the odds, his pick was nothing short of incredible.[20]

Tulane University Coach Cliff Wells expressed his own thoughts about the final game in an article written by Shelbyville News Sports Editor, Bill Holtel. "That final game shooting by Shelbyville was the most amazing exhibition I have even seen in high school. Had I not taken a second look, I would have sworn it was Rupp's Kentucky Wonders. This made the 37th finals I have seen. Haven't missed one yet!"

The finale of the celebration period was a huge parade staged on Wednesday, April 2, 1947. Touted as the largest event in the city's history, the parade included more than two hundred floats and marching bands. All schools closed in preparation for the evening's activities. The Eagles Lodge hosted a dinner for the team before the parade.

When the parade ended at the Public Square, fans were treated to an elaborate public program presented from the bunting-draped balcony of the Hotel Shelby. Later, a dance at the local National Guard Armory entertained hundreds of county high school students until one o'clock in the morning.

Overall, the episode proved to be a "once in a lifetime" experience for the community. Never again did one of its teams win the title, although a few came very, very close. Those coming closest lost in either the Semi-State or the State Final round of the nationally famous "one class, winner-take-all" high school basketball tournament.

Hetty Gray

In 1947, for the first time in its history, Shelbyville High School chose more than one player to receive The Paul Cross Award. Players Bill Breck, Bill Garrett, Loren Hemingway, Emerson Johnson, and Marshall Murray shared the award. That year, the committee honored the senior complement on the 1947 Indiana High School State Championship Golden Bears. Selection criteria mandated the highest levels of scholarship, leadership, team play, and sportsmanship.

Today, in retrospect, surviving team members credit their coaching staff for tremendous guidance during their high school years. There is no doubt that Coach Barnett and Coach Barnes stressed the fine points of the game. But, more importantly, the 1947 players state unequivocally that the two men taught by pure example. They led impeccable lives, both personally and professionally.

Men of ideal character, the pair stood out as role models for the young men in their care. Although the Golden Bears were not an anomaly in terms of the team's racial mix, the group did stand out in one aspect — the trio of talented Negro varsity starters in a predominately white high school was unique in Hoosier basketball at the time.

Fans in the stands, and players and coaches on the benches, often screamed ugly, racial slurs at Negro players in the 1940s. Their behavior, compounded by fact that their acts went virtually unpunished, threw a moral pall over the entire sport. Irregardless of the roles of those who ignored the situation, or condoned it — the end result was the same. Officials did not step up to the plate and condemn the open, public discrimination of Negroes. Instead, they did nothing.

That fact alone set Frank Barnes and "Doc" Barnett apart from their peers. Coach Barnes had his own way to handle the problem. His reaction to open discrimination had a profound impact on the lives of his players. He recognized the need to support his players emotionally, and he did just that.

Bill's character strengthened during high school. Fellow players saw him excoriated by angry fans at out of town games, and they were awed by his reaction. Bill's inner strength, buoyed by a fierce independence and sense of self-worth, insulated him from the rude remarks of those around him. His emotional and psychological armor protected him whenever he donned his uniform. An unyielding inner strength enabled the shy teenager to completely block out the crowd during a game.

Endless insults might have crushed other players his age, but they did nothing to deter him from his main focus — the game. When an opponent uttered vicious comments to his face, Bill gave no indication that he even heard the words. Instead, his cool attitude actually seemed to increase in tandem with the degree of the opponent's insults.

In essence, his reaction disarmed a would-be intimidator of any power to affect his level of play. To many onlookers, it was plain that Bill's Christian faith played a part. What they witnessed was a real-life, 1940s rendition of "turning the other cheek."

Yet, the crux of his demeanor was true character. A man long before age chronicled him as such, Bill Garrett was perhaps the best-prepared of any Negro high school basketball player in the nation to make what would be heralded a tremendous inroad in established collegiate sports.

Indiana honored Bill as 1947 "Mr. Basketball" and named him to the 1947 Indiana All-Stars, who practiced over the summer and played against other like teams. Ever the consummate competitor, Bill continued to amass fans across the Midwest.

Bill Garrett shone as a candle in the darkness. Consistent and calm when faced with harsh, outward forces, he burned brightly within — fueled by an immense depth of personal pride and self-worth — the products of a good and loving family. Such personal qualities anchored him well as he matured, and they would continue to gird him as a new, and unexpected, chapter opened in his life.

Chapter Eight

Of the players on the 1947 Championship Golden Bear team, three seniors went on to college and not only became high school teachers, but also coaches. In addition, Walter Wintin, a junior member of the Bear squad, had a very successful teaching and coaching career at Seymour High School for many years. His comments on the events that led Bill Garrett toward a career in college basketball provide valuable, and insightful, background material.

According to Wintin, "High school basketball officials managed the game at a level typical of the time. Foul calls were much more relaxed then. I know now that I was much too naïve to realize the degree of discrimination aimed at the Negro players on our team, especially Bill Garrett. The referees controlled the game, but not strictly.

"In one particular instance against East Chicago Washington, I saw a player cut back on Bill sharply. Bill went down very hard, but after a few seconds, he rose and walked to the other end of the floor and sunk two free throws, swishing the net with typical ease."

The times and the atmosphere were far different in the 1940s. It never occurred to anyone on the Golden Bear squad to verbally defend a teammate. In that time period, society sidestepped poor treatment of Negroes as a group, and very few judged the majority silence as condoning the ill treatment. No one incident compelled the white populace to take action, and conversely, no formal movement existed to protect the Negroes' rights

Given time, the situation was bound to change, but in 1947, things remained at a virtual standstill in terms of improving race relations. However, despite the fact that it maintained a good reputation with regard to its Negro residents, Shelbyville, too, was guilty of some degrees of discrimination. Sadly, even in Bill's hometown, a few places existed where Negroes were not welcome.

Nationwide, feelings began to rise among the Negro population, but it would be years before it reached a level from which the modern Civil Rights movement would grow. For the time, Shelbyville was progressive, and, insofar as it could be, far more permissive than the communities and counties surrounding it.

In one county to the east, signs of "No Niggers" were common, and in one particular community it was a well known fact that Negroes were neither tolerated or welcomed, even if only passing through town. Passive acceptance and tolerance of the blatant mistreatment was a blame that could be laid at the feet of all those involved — both Negro and white.

It was against this background that one Shelbyville businessman took a firm stand and pushed for Bill Garrett to enter the door still firmly closed to Negro athletes — the door to collegiate competition.

That local man, Nate Kaufman, was a highly respected, experienced IHSAA official, and he took a keen interest in Bill Garrett's future prospects. Kaufman loved the game of basketball. Coincidentally, the two shared a common bond that dated to their days in high school, even though decades separated them in terms of age. Both Kaufman and Garrett won the Paul Cross Award — Kaufman in 1922 and Garrett in both 1946 and 1947. Because Kaufman played basketball at both the "semi-pro" and "pro" levels for ten years, he had a wealth of experience at every level of play.

In addition to playing basketball, Kaufman also coached the sport. During his first year as head coach at St. Joseph's High School, his team gained a berth in The National Catholic Basketball Tournament. In terms of officiating Hoosier basketball, Kaufman officiated five straight Indiana high school state title games from 1936 to 1940 — a distinctive credit for an IHSAA referee.

A select series of events blended toward achieving what portended to be an inaccessible goal. Kaufman approached a man of vision, a man who helped lay the groundwork for a dramatic transformation in Bloomington. Enter Indiana University President of eleven years, Herman B Wells.

At the same time, Wells was waging his own private battle against discrimination aimed at Negro students on campus. In truth, his moves were not received positively by the Negro community itself. It was no secret that catering to the Negro students was a lucrative business, but with the help of the NAACP and prominent Negro alumni in Indianapolis, he saw that the barriers came down.

Wells, a highly ethical man, who accepted the reins of Indiana in 1938, took a great interest in all areas of college life, including collegiate sports. So, when he decided to open the swimming pool to Negroes on campus, he did so with flair. According to Wells, in his 1980 book, *Being Lucky*, that move was made through IU's Athletic Director, Zora Clevenger.

Wells inquired as to when the pool was most crowded. Clevenger replied that pool use was at its zenith in the afternoons, between 2:30 and 4:30 PM. Pondering that information, Wells then asked Clevenger to name the most popular Negro athlete on campus. That answer was easy: "Rooster

Coffee," a football player with a lively personality, who had won the heart of the entire campus.

Wells asked if "Rooster" was in the building in the afternoon, and Clevenger replied that he worked out afternoons on a regular basis. Upon Wells' instructions, Clevenger was to keep the plan secret. Since students swam in the nude for sanitary reasons, Clevenger was to ask "Rooster" to strip down and jump in for a swim in the varsity pool.

Wells admonished Clevenger to not tell a soul what he was going to do in advance, and that included "Rooster." A few days later, "Rooster" slipped into the pool and swam, in Wells' words, "with abandon" for a half an hour or so. In the midst of the scene, Wells and Clevenger doubted if any of the students realized that a policy had been changed. That day ended the discrimination at the IU pool.[21]

Wells was determined to see that all students enjoyed equal treatment, but he had not yet addressed the conference-wide policy of the basketball programs. Given his mindset, the gregarious administrator plowed fertile ground for those who sought to plant a new seed of opportunity for Negro athletes.

It was in this vein that Wells, the administrator, played a key role in the next phase of Bill Garrett's life. Since no letters of intent existed during that period, high school players had no requirement to sign on with colleges actively recruiting players. In contrast to today's formal arrangements, the standard procedures of the 1940s included a plethora of "under the table antics." With no governing rules, coaches were left to their own devices.

In Wells' own words, "At that time there was an informal understanding among the basketball coaches that now seems incredible. There was some kind of mumbo jumbo about the fact that the sport included too much bodily contact to make it feasible to mix the races.

"One day in the spring (1947), some of my Black friends from Indianapolis, many of whom were alumni, showed up in my office to say that if our basketball coach, Branch McCracken, would play Bill Garrett, they felt that they could persuade him to come to Indiana University. Bill Garrett had a fabulous record as a high school player, and his team had just won the state tournament. I said, 'That would be great. Let me see what I can do.'"[22]

Wells held out high hopes for breaking the so-called "color barrier" in college basketball, but he remained stoic in one respect — his number one consideration was recruiting a player with ability. Talent was the paramount requisite of Wells' search, and Kaufman assured Wells that Bill embodied extraordinary talent.

When Wells spoke to Clevenger, the Athletic Director voiced a sticking point on behalf of the conference — scheduling games. Clevenger feared that recruiting a Negro player could jeopardize Indiana's entire program. "But," he added, "if Branch wants to do it, I'll back him."

In the summer of 1947, President Wells went to McCracken on behalf of Bill Garrett. Wells, acutely aware that never in its history had Indiana University recruited a Negro player for its basketball program, spent considerable time discussing the possibility of such a move with Indiana's head basketball coach.

Wells asked McCracken if he would like to have Bill Garrett on his team, and this was his enthusiastic reply: "That would be great. He's a magnificent basketball player and we sure could use him, but you know I probably would be ostracized by all my fellow Big Ten coaches if we took him."

Replied Wells, "Let's take him, and if there's any conference backlash against it, then I'll take the responsibility for handling it."

McCracken was silent.

Wells moved to convince the head coach, saying "In the first place, they won't dare make a public issue of it, and if they harass you in private, I will, through the Council of Ten, bring the pressure of the other nine Big Ten presidents to bear on the coaches."[23]

Although Bill Garrett's route to Indiana University included many twists and turns, first-person interviews with family members of those personally involved in the process confirm that those involved were both Negro and white. These men and their zeal for change overcame what were, at that time, considered impossible odds.

While Wells was making his moves with his athletic staff, Kaufman and his friends plunged headlong into their own personal quest for athletic parity. He personally pushed to convince collegiate officials to keep the most talented Hoosier high school players in the State of Indiana. He wanted the brightest and most talented high school players to remain within their home state to play college basketball. Kaufman saw no valid reason why Hoosier colleges failed to recruit Indiana's talented Negro players. To him, losing these athletes to other state colleges and universities was an inexcusable mistake.

At that time, the "Big Nine" Conference, to which Indiana University belonged, did not enroll Negro players into their basketball programs. Track and football programs accepted Negro players, but basketball did not.

Johnny Wilson, standout player on the 1946 Indiana State Championship Anderson Indians, went out of state to play collegiate basketball. In the wake of that loss, Kaufman's protestations encouraged other notable Hoosiers to join with him in a crusade to change the entire process.

Many college scouts spotted Bill Garrett early, as did Negro fans. Indianapolis' Crispus Attucks High School maintained very close ties to a number of Negro colleges in the South. While it might have seemed alien to the majority of Indiana high schools, Attucks had good reason to pursue such ties. That reason was one of pure necessity. In the absence of truly open competition, the administrators and athletic officials at Attucks were forced to secure competitive arenas for their players, despite their locations.

Attucks basketball teams traveled to Negro campuses in the South for many years before they were allowed to compete with other Indianapolis high schools. The link with those colleges not only inspired Attucks students to higher education, but, more to the point, it also exposed Indiana's Negro players to college scouts.

Reflecting this pattern, in 1946 and 1947, a number of those same Southern Negro colleges concentrated on a graceful, accomplished, 6-foot 2-inch, high school basketball center from Shelbyville, Indiana. Most basketball fans resigned themselves to the sad fact that Bill, like Johnny, would be forced to leave Indiana to play college ball.

Meanwhile, "behind the scenes" actions and meetings resulted in swift progress. Kaufman's considerable influence in high school basketball meshed with that of others. Finally, en masse, their pleas formed an undergirding, grassroots support for what Wells and Clevenger saw as the future of Big Ten Basketball.

In the end, on behalf of Shelbyville's star center, a committed core of Hoosier men forged a signature change in the recruiting procedures for collegiate basketball.

Kaufman's son, Bart, an Indianapolis businessman, confirms that his father worked closely with President Wells, Coach McCracken, as well as many others, in the drive to recruit Bill Garrett to play basketball at Indiana University.

A crucial point is that, at that time, the prospect of recruiting a Negro basketball player held many pitfalls. Conference schools routinely played Negroes in other sports, including football and track, yet no member school had a Negro on its basketball team. The usual consequence was a migration of the best Negro basketball players to out-of-state colleges and universities. For a time, it looked as if Bill Garrett would be among the lost elite.

Following the lead of his peers, the head coach of Tennessee State drove north to Shelbyville in late summer of 1947, picked up Bill Garrett at his home, and drove the young man back to Nashville, Tennessee. The 1947 Indiana State Championship only intensified the Negro colleges' interest in Bill. For all intents and purposes, it appeared that another Hoosier basketball star was destined to shine in another state.

Simultaneously, after much ferment in the meetings at IU, a decision came forth. In one of the final meetings, Kaufman made a pointed inquiry of McCracken.

"Are you going to play him? Is he good enough?" asked Kaufman.

"Yes, I'll play him. He's good enough for me." McCracken replied.

That brief, three sentence, two-person exchange set in motion a series of phone calls that resulted in Bill's abrupt return to the State of Indiana, and, ultimately, earned him a place in Hoosier sports history.

Media sources were slow to digest what was happening, and several articles in major state papers questioned if IU really would sign Bill. For example, The April 17, 1997, issue of *The Indiana Daily Student* declared that McCracken wanted Garrett, but the veteran coach was fearful that having a Negro team member would complicate scheduling games with competing schools. In the end, Coach McCracken's "presumed" worries proved to be totally groundless.

Chapter Nine

In the era of media hype we encounter today, the arrival of a highly rated, incoming freshman collegiate athlete prompts a press entourage and an official university reception committee. However, those employed in print and broadcast media of the late 1940s exhibited little resemblance to present-day, high profile, celebrity-status sports commentators.

Armed with sound trucks and a veritable entourage of technicians, today's sports reporters brandish their microphones without restraint. These sportscaster versions of "paparazzi" systematically "dog" the steps of today's talented freshman draft picks under consideration by large colleges and universities.

In contrast, the scene when Bill Garrett arrived in Bloomington didn't begin to replicate that kind of drama. In fact, his arrival was anything but spectacular. The sundry passengers who traveled south on Indiana State Road 37 that day in 1947 were completely oblivious to the identity of the quiet, tall youngster who accompanied them. Nobody noticed anything unusual as he ambled up the aisle toward the door of the silver coach and stood patiently while the uniformed driver retrieved his suitcase.

When Bill Garrett climbed off the Greyhound Bus in downtown Bloomington that day in 1947, he drew little attention from people inside the depot or outside on the sidewalk. More importantly, no university personnel welcomed him.

Bill glanced at a note in his hand, picked up his luggage, and walked up West Kirkwood. Once he crossed Indiana, he stood before the impressive stone gate at the edge of the heavily wooded campus. Indiana University boasted many limestone buildings, some of which were covered with ivy. Their leaded glass windows glistened in the sunshine. Shaded by huge trees, wide sidewalks wound among the stately buildings. As first impressions went, Indiana must have made a good one, because, in many people's minds, the campus looked much more "Ivy League" than Midwestern.

Following his written instructions, Bill walked across campus and reported to Coach Branch McCracken. Later that day, he moved into Hoosier Halls, a residential facility physically attached to the fieldhouse. There, in the company of the other Negro athletes, he unpacked his belongings and began college life. University housing posed a problem for Negro students, especially the male athletes. In response, IU designated Hoosier Halls as the housing unit specifically for them.

Coaches and faculty watched Bill with interest, yet the person most instrumental for Bill's enrollment faced a surprising interruption in his normal routine. Shortly after Bill began classes at IU, President Herman B Wells suddenly left the Indiana University campus. Federal officials convinced Wells to serve six months as an educational and cultural advisor in occupied Germany.

Although his service to his country pre-empted his official duties, Wells — ever the dedicated administrator — maintained close contact ties with Bloomington.

Although no personal papers documented that Wells kept track of Bill's progress at IU, few on campus doubted the President's sincere, and continuing, interest in the young player who broke the color barrier in the "Big Nine." The term, "Big Nine," rings alien today, but it stands correct for the time cited.

Prior to Bill's enrollment at IU in the fall of 1947, the University of Chicago had withdrawn from the Big Ten, and Michigan State had not yet signed on as a member. In 1947, the Big Nine Conference schools were Indiana, Illinois, Ohio State, Michigan, Wisconsin, Minnesota, Purdue, Iowa, and Northwestern. That level of competition was perfectly suited for Indiana's reigning "Mr. Basketball," although he would never have voiced such a claim himself. Bill's talent spoke for itself, and true to form, he remained characteristically quiet and shy.

Bill's full class schedule supported his major in physical education and minor in business. He never missed a class or a practice session. Freshman competition was fierce, and Bill worked very hard to improve his skills. After weeks of hard work, of the 120 candidates, Branch McCracken chose Bill and ten others for the freshman basketball team's starting lineup.

Eleven more players rounded out the freshman roster for the 1947-48 season. Bill's All-State status as center on Shelbyville's team garnered a great deal of attention from critical members of the coaching staff. Characteristically, his attitude was consistent, and he acted as if he were no better or worse than any one else on the squad. His personality drew fellow students to him. In no time, the entire student body embraced the lithe, talented athlete, and their warm campus welcome heartened him.

Negro students met in one particular area of the massive Student Union Building. Actually, at one time the tables were labeled "Reserved." Everyone in the dining hall knew what the signs meant, but they really bothered President Wells, who felt that the signage was nothing short of a corporate insult. As a result, he acted very swiftly. James Patrick, Manager of the Union Building, removed the signs in an "unobtrusive" manner, on the direction of Wells. It was two weeks before anyone noticed that the signs were gone, and then, according to Wells, "the absurdity of the previous situation was apparent."[24]

Negro students continued to meet in that same area of The Commons, comfortable in familiar surroundings, but, pleasantly, absent the signs. There, gathered around several tables, the young people not only developed close friendships, but they also planned their social activities. On common ground, they created a society within a society, and, in the process, forged alliances and close friendships that lasted a lifetime.

Less than ten percent of the total student population on campus, the Negro collegians took it upon themselves to create their own social calendar. Many male students lived off campus or in Hoosier Halls, and coeds lived in dorms. Few Negro facilities existed where large groups could assemble, so the Negro sponsored Greek organizations filled that gap, and their houses often hosted weekend parties.

The spirited, weekday banter that peppered the Union in impromptu meetings failed to draw Bill's participation when he began to sit in with the group. As a general rule, he seldom entered into conversation. The other students noticed his silence, but nobody prodded him to interact. Instead, they simply allowed him to sit back and listen as they discussed a wide variety of subjects.

His sophomore year, Bill started for "The Hurryin' Hoosiers." After completing his stint on the freshman team with flying colors, he looked forward to his next full college season on the varsity. However, in the athletic offices, Coach

McCracken voiced his concern about Bill's grades. For that reason, over the course of the summer, Coach McCracken planned a complete change of scene for his talented center.

Fate intervened in Bill Garrett's life during the 1947-48 academic year. He emerged from his freshman year a stronger and a far more savvy player. Coach McCracken held out high hopes for his young protégé, and expressed his own brand of intuitive enthusiasm in several interviews with area sportswriters.

By December 1948, Bill's name became more and more common in sports columns statewide. However, the most succinct coverage came from *The Indiana Daily Student*, Bloomington's best source for reliable campus information. The December 14th issue featured this headline: "Future Looks Bright for Garrett and for I.U."

McCracken knew all too well that many of the athletes who lived in Hoosier Halls failed to make high grades. Since the coach held his own personal academic expectations for his players, he was convinced that Bill would take classes seriously if he lived in a setting more conducive to studying.

McCracken's fears that his rising star might fall prey to the same sort of inattention fueled his search for Bill's new accommodations. The "movers and shakers" on campus recognized McCracken's reputation as a keen observer of the student body. Further, they knew that the coach had a firm grasp of exactly which individual athletes were succeeding or failing. Intent on assuring Bill's academic success, McCracken scoured the area for suitable housing to replace the social milieu of Hoosier Halls.

After much consideration and investigation, McCracken concentrated on excellent male Negro students at IU. After a thorough investigation of men, the coach noted the achievement of one student in particular, a Negro pre-med student, who roomed in a local home. An older student, the talented man was just the mentor that McCracken sought for his blue-ribbon player.

After speaking to the student's host family, McCracken secured Bill a room in the residence. Soon after classes began, Bill moved into the home of Russell and Betty Johnson at 1222 North Madison. Russell worked as a shoemaker, and Betty was a homemaker. The Russells had no children, and they welcomed the college students as pleasant additions to their home. In short, they treated the young men as their "family."

The older, undergraduate student who lived with the Russells was a veteran attending school on the G. I. Bill. The older man's influence would prove to have a profound effect on Bill Garrett, the student. In essence, James Roberson was "just what the doctor ordered" years before he had earned his own medical degree.

After the conclusion of World War II, Roberson visited many campuses. He looked for a medical school that openly welcomed Negro students. He witnessed many instances of discrimination in restaurants near those colleges he visited, but few of them involved bothered to take the situation seriously. In the end, he judged IU "OK," and immediately enrolled at the scenic Bloomington campus.

The son of devoted parents, Roberson was one of six children in college at the same time. Military service delayed his college experience, and, as a result, he and his siblings all attended college simultaneously. James' parents shared values in common with Leon and Laura Garrett. The two couples both prized a college education as the most important goal for their children.

Like Laura Garrett, James' mother worked as a domestic. However, the family for whom she worked was extremely influential. Mrs. Roberson worked for the DuPonts. When James sought to enter the armed forces in World War II, he yearned to be a "Tuskegee Airman." However, Tuskegee Institute required two years of college for all of its applicants.

When James' mother mentioned the problem to the DuPonts, they decided to intercede on his behalf. After investigating the situation, the DuPonts secured an agreement for James' admission, with the caveat of a high score on the entrance exam scheduled for July 23, 1943. He excelled on the exam, and by December, Tuskegee accepted James for its acclaimed aviation program.

James ranked fourth or fifth among all the former collegians in his class. After completing his training in Florida and Texas, he was certified as a bombardier/navigator. Even as a member of such an elite group, James encountered bias and discrimination. Many of his military experiences with discrimination paralleled Bill Garrett's encounters while playing high school basketball. When the two men were introduced at the Johnson home that fall day in 1948, neither of them realized how much they had in common, despite the difference in their ages.

Dr. Roberson remembers the first time he met Bill Garrett. In his words, "I was face to face with a bright-eyed young man, full of athletic ability. The fellow had an easy-going personality."

Within weeks, Bill's routine changed. After class or practice, instead of walking back into a party atmosphere, Bill returned to his room where his roommate studied. The habit became contagious. In short order, Bill adopted a more serious attitude toward homework, and by the end of the first semester of his sophomore year, his grades reflected his increased effort.

Dr. Roberson commented that Bill excelled, especially

when pushed. He didn't find that surprising, considering Bill's attitude on the basketball court. The harder the game, the harder he played. Pressure spurred Bill to previously unattained heights. In time, Roberson grew very proud of his roommate and watched his progress in pure awe.

In Roberson's junior year, one of his professors suggested that he compete for a Rhodes Scholarship. Roberson worked hard toward the goal, but withdrew from the competition, because he wanted one of the openings to the IU School of Medicine. It was a hard decision, but one based on financial considerations.

Roberson lacked the funding of his fellow pre-med students. His decision to drop out of the Rhodes competition hinged solely on the fact that four of the six positions open in the medical school were partially funded. The choice was particularly critical to him, because he was confident that he had a lock on one position in particular — an opening in biology and embryology. When the announcements were made, he was on the list. His decision, albeit bittersweet, had been the correct one.

Influenced by his roommate's rigorous study schedule, star IU basketball player, Bill Garrett, "hit the books." When McCracken investigated Bill's grades, he credited Roberson with the progress. Unlike the case with many other student athletes, academic eligibility never posed a problem for Bill Garrett, college athlete.

The old adage, "You can judge a man by the company he keeps," truly applied to Bill Garrett, the student. The company Bill kept, in the person of a determined, studious roommate, paid great dividends. Dr. Roberson stated that Bill saw — first-hand — the fruits of his own labor, in terms of a grade point average.

While they roomed together, the two men forged a deep,

lasting friendship. Roberson's sense of commitment and dedication made an impression on Bill. Moreover, Bill's steady, grounded personality impressed his older roommate. Extremely slow to anger, Bill accepted adversity and challenge in silence.

Instead of surrendering to wrath, Bill internalized his thoughts and retreated into his own private world. His attitude inspired respect in his fellow students. In the words of Coach McCracken's widow, Mary Jo McCracken, "everyone fell in love with Garrett — at least everyone in Bloomington."[25]

Chapter Ten

When critiquing Bill's freshman record at IU, Columnist Charlie Teeple predicted that Bill's "Mr. Indiana High School Basketball" title of 1947 could reach a parallel honor at the college level, "Mr. Indiana College Basketball," within the upcoming three years. Teeple based his projection on Garrett's "cat-like playing." Sharpening the skills he demonstrated at the high school level, Bill leaped around the college court with amazing agility, consistently throwing his opponents off their game.

Bill's varsity career took off like a rocket. In the first four games of the season, Bill emerged as the Hurryin' Hoosiers' third best scorer, quite an achievement considering the other members of the starting five. Bill adapted to his forward position with diligence. Meshing beautifully with his fellow players, his exceptional ball handling went a long way to further McCracken's team in its quest for conference honors. When Illinois opened the Big Nine season at the IU Fieldhouse in January, the Illini squad faced a Hoosier team ranked fourth in the nation.

The Hoosiers' trip to Madison for a game against Wisconsin's Badgers issued in an entirely new experience for Bill Garrett — air travel. As the plane lifted off from Weir Cook Airport in Indianapolis on a cold January afternoon bound for Madison's Badger lair on the shore of Lake

Mendota, the usually calm nineteen-year-old was extremely nervous about the flight, and his comments reflected his mood.

Tom Miller, IU's Sports Information Director, accompanied the team on that flight. Miller claimed one of his favorite memories of Bill stemmed from that airplane ride. His words, reported in a major university publication dated March 7, 1986, recounted their exchange.

"During one of our road trips, the team took a DC-3. It was pretty bumpy and it was Bill's first plane ride. Coach McCracken noticed that Bill seemed a little nervous and went over and said, 'Bill, there's no use in worrying. When your number is up, that's it.' Bill's response was, 'Coach, what's worrying me is — what if the pilot's number is up?'"

Bill was always one to think ahead and assess a situation from every possible angle. His smile never gave a hint of his most private thoughts. To all observers, he met life on its own terms, but in his own way. His inner composure steeled him for the reception he faced at "away games" across the Midwest.

If Bill felt the pressure of his position as the first Negro in the Big Ten, his teammates never noticed. Some of them attribute their inattention to naiveté. Even in terms of campus activities, Bill shied away from any parties. However, that reluctant attitude took a sudden turn one day the second semester of his sophomore year, when he sauntered to a spot among those who gathered in the Union Building.

Bill joined the group of Negro students who sat at a long table in The Commons that day. As usual, he listened quietly as the others chatted among themselves. For some reason, he raised his eyes and glanced down the table. Suddenly, his eyes met those of a lovely young woman. Immediately, a smile spread across her face.

He hadn't noticed her before, so he wondered if she were

new on campus. Over a period of a few weeks, the two of them began to talk. Betty Guess was a junior, but she missed the first semester of the school year. Due to a family emergency, Betty had sacrificed one semester of college to stay at home and care for her ailing mother.

Betty's lively personality captivated Bill. In contrast, his shyness drew him to her. They enjoyed a few dates by June. It was common to see the couple walking to services at Bloomington's West Side Baptist Church. Bill called her several times that summer, but he made no commitment to her. She never questioned his motives, because he made his priorities clear early in their relationship. Basketball and class came first; friends and social life came second. During his sophomore year, his active role on the varsity basketball team consumed much of his time.

It was evident to everyone on campus that, during that time, Bill Garrett's rapport with Indiana University's student body deepened. Indiana students respected Bill, and they made no attempt to keep their feelings under wraps. When he stepped onto the floor at home games, the roar of the crowd said it all. The partisan, Hoosier crowd not only respected him as a player, but they absolutely adored him as a person.

Betty's dorm, Elms Hall, enforced an early curfew on weeknights, so she, like most of the other coeds, dated only on weekends. Fraternity parties consisted of simple entertainment. The fellows rolled up the rugs, someone carried in a record player, and an assigned spokesman invited guests to get up and dance.

A physical education major, Betty Guess aspired to coach — a career goal ingrained early in her youth in Southern Indiana. She graduated from Broadway High School, a segregated facility in Madison, Indiana. Broadway High School was the first colored high school commissioned in the State of Indiana in 1898. Because no IHSAA venues were open to her high school, Betty's high school sports credentials rested solely on intramural contests. She never attended an integrated school until she enrolled at Indiana University. A determined individual, she aimed for both undergraduate and post-graduate degrees to prepare her for a successful life as a teacher and a coach.

When she and Bill met, they both had firm career plans. Both of them were intent on making excellent grades in order to have an opportunity to secure good jobs after graduation. Given their common mindset, when Bill placed their personal relationship on "a back burner" until after the basketball season, Betty understood perfectly.

The couple attended dances together, but they never espoused, or encouraged, a serious relationship with anyone else. Betty worked part time at the main library on campus, and when she could afford a ticket, she went to home games. She genuinely enjoyed watching Bill play. Crowd reaction in the IU Fieldhouse impressed Betty.

She was extremely proud of Bill's conduct on the court. Word spread about the slurs hurled at Bill when the team played on the road. Betty winced, but she was not shocked at the reports. She had encountered discrimination as a child, and she knew how it hurt. However, in spite the travails of his pioneering position, Bill broke through the invisible curtain of bias and bigotry. When he entered into the realm of the Big Ten Basketball, he did it with style.

In reference to collegiate basketball's unspoken racial obstacle of that time, Tom Miller couldn't fathom why the barrier even existed. For years, Negro athletes had played football and run track in conference schools. Miller attributed basketball's racial roadblock to the fact that basketball was considered an extremely intimate sport, compared to either football or track and field.

McCracken's courage in playing Bill Garrett soon prompted the other Big Ten coaches to sign Negro players. The NAACP awarded Coach Branch McCracken a watch for breaking the racial barrier in The Big Ten Conference.

After his freshman and sophomore years, Bill's talents increased to a level that rewarded him with collegiate honors — both at IU and in the entire conference. His performance not only delighted the fans, but it also validated Indiana's trend-setting decision to recruit him.

During Bill's junior year, he invited Betty to go to his home to meet his family over Spring Break. She made another visit again that the summer. Bill's parents welcomed Betty. They endeared themselves to her, and in turn, she to them. Further, Betty really enjoyed the company of Bill's two younger sisters. That school year was a good one for the two of them, in terms of their relationship. Betty was a senior, and she and Bill began to consider their future seriously.

After graduation, Betty accepted a job at The Phyllis Wheatley YWCA on West Street in Indianapolis. Because of the physical distance between them, their absences grew more painful by the month. Weekends found one or the other on the road. However, Betty made many more trips, due to Bill's tight game schedule.

The student body adored Bill Garrett during his years at IU. Unfortunately, that level of acceptance failed to extend beyond the borders of the Bloomington campus. Racial bias reared its angry head when the college team played away from home. Hotel managers were no more hospitable when Bill was in college than the restaurant owners had been when he was in high school.

In one particular instance, the hotel manager made it clear to Coach McCracken that Garrett would have to stay in a room by himself. Clearly irritated by the bigoted attitude, McCracken replied that any player on his team was perfectly willing to share a room with Bill.

Once the team arrived, the manager insisted that the entire team enter the hotel by the back stairs. In addition, he ordered his staff to bar Bill from eating in the dining room with the rest of his teammates. On that note, the team made its own plans. After a scouting mission among the local eateries, players settled on an Irish place. The owner welcomed the group warmly, saying, "Sure, bring him in. I'm just over from the old country and a stranger myself." [26]

Betty appreciated the fact that Bill's teammates were highly protective of him in the face of ill treatment. Although the entire Hoosier team was prepared to defend Bill when necessary, Phil Buck, Gene Ring, and Bill Tosheff took the lead — forming the tight, consistent inner circle that supported the shy, talented player.

Today, Bill Tosheff lives in San Diego, California. His memories give a view of Bill from a player's perspective.

"As individuals, none of us were really superstars, but we did gel as a team. Bill was a fine fellow…a good friend…a tenacious competitor…a class act….To put his ability into two words, I would say that Bill Garrett was quietly lethal."

Senior Manager George Vlassis had responsibilities ranging from making sure all the equipment was in good condition to handling the money on team trips. The money situation itself is comical today, given present-day allegiances to credit cards, receipts, and Palm Pilots. George had his own method. He carried all the team money around in a paper bag.

Privy to conversations, both on the bench and among the players, George noted how the team blended into a cohesive unit on and off the court. Moreover, George respected Bill

Garrett for both his talent and his demeanor. To this day, George remembers Bill's tremendous personality and talent. He considers him a model athlete.

Sam Esposito also played for IU. Today, he is retired and lives in Raleigh, North Carolina. When asked about Bill, he replied with enthusiasm.

"I only knew Bill for a short time. I started at IU in the spring semester of 1951, Bill's senior year — actually, his last semester to play for the Hurryin' Hoosiers. Because I was a lowly freshman, I could only participate in scrimmage games against the varsity squad. I watched him carefully. It seemed to me that the elements of play came easily for him. To me, he was a natural athlete and a great player.

"He was a very quiet guy. He led through example and displayed a great deal of class. Everyone on the team liked him. I only regret that I came along too late to actually play with him and really to get to know him on a more personal level."

Ernie Andres served as Assistant Indiana University Basketball Coach under Branch McCracken. Andres remembers all too well the nasty scenes of college play when Bill played for Indiana. His vivid recollections paint a less than flattering portrait of Bill's reception, both on and off the basketball court, when he began to play for the Hurryin' Hoosiers. Andres' words not only further clarify the situation, they also provide an inside view from the IU bench.

"What Bill Garrett went through as a member of the Indiana University basketball team was more than any human being should have had to endure. He was abused mentally, physically, and verbally, but he never did lose his cool. His courage and self-control were amazing. I would call Bill 'the Jackie Robinson of Big Ten Basketball.'

"Bill was a great player and, as a center, he had to compete against much bigger men. He always handled these assignments quite well. He was a fine team player and well liked by his coaches and teammates. You never had to worry about his grades, as he was a good student.

"By the time Bill was a senior at IU, he was not only admired by the Hoosier fans, coaches, and players, but also by opposing fans. Bill was a courageous young man and a gentleman all the way."

Bill's close friend, Gene Ring is also retired and makes his home in Indianapolis, Indiana. His memories of Bill echo those of other players, yet they exude their own unique perspective.

"During the 1950-51 season, our basketball team held a record of nineteen wins and three losses. Bill Garrett was instrumental for that great season. 'Hurryin' Hoosier' was what Bill Garrett represented. Bill had the respect of his teammates. He always had a soft handshake, accompanied by a smile. He had a good sense of humor. I especially remember his giggle. We shared a friendship, and he was always the same man I met for the first time at IU one day in 1947."

In his three-year career on the varsity Hoosier basketball team, Bill was named IU's Most Valuable Player. In addition, he earned All-Conference and All-American honors. At the end of his senior year, The IU Hurryin' Hoosiers' record of 19 and 3 positioned them very high in national college standings. Because IU ranked No. 2 and No. 7 on the major wire services, Coach McCracken's crew had every reason to be proud.

IU had come a long way in the years following 1948, a year in which it suffered a losing season. An article in the March/April, 1998, issue of *Indiana Alumni Magazine* cited "that season ended —and not coincidentally — as the last Big Ten Conference team composed exclusively of white basketball players. Garrett stepped into a place in history that Indiana University had set aside for him the summer before as the first black, full scholarship basketball player in the premier athletic conference in America."

The publication continued. "Garrett not only wore the mantle admirably, he excelled. From his first game as a sophomore, he made the starting lineup and led the team to records of 14-8, 17-5, and 19-3. As a senior, he made numerous All-American teams."

Quoting teammate, and the third member of the "invincible Garrett triangle," Phil Buck, "Bill must have been closer to 6-2 than 6-3, but he was so agile. He had such finesse. He played smarter basketball than most guys did. That's the worst thing that can happen to a big guy, you know — to have to guard someone smaller and quicker.

"I met Bill for the first time in the summer of 1947 when we both played on the Indiana High School All Stars. We roomed together at the YMCA and had a great time. We both ended up at Bloomington, and during our freshman year, we'd slip into the IU Fieldhouse on Sundays to shoot baskets.

"That was all the entertainment we could afford. Neither of us had any money. So, when Coach McCracken called me in and asked me if I would room with Bill when we went on the road, I said, 'Heavens, yes, he's one of my best buddies.'"

That reply, in the wake of what was happening around the nation at that time, reflected the solid values of the Hoosier players.

Bill's surprise arrival at IU, like any controversial move in athletics, brought with it many questions as to the motives of those involved with his recruitment. Reporters were not lax in pushing their agendas, and often approached the players themselves for a pithy quote.

Bill Tosheff was asked once if he thought that

Shelbyville's Nate Kaufman was out "to make history." Tosheff restated his reply as if he uttered it only yesterday. To the questioner, he said, "I knew Nate, and I'm not sure he was even aware that Bill would actually be the *first* Negro player in the Big Ten. I think he was just extremely loyal to a Shelbyville player. Nate recognized in Bill a tremendous talent that could really benefit Indiana University."

Teammate, Gene Ring: " I played with a lot of Negroes in high school at South Bend Central, so I never even thought about color." Continuing, he remarked about how Bill was often on the heavy end of the 'ribbing stick.'

"Bill's naiveté earned him some merciless ribbing at the hands of his teammates. We took the train to Minnesota. We got there a day early — during their game the day before. We went to the arena and could hear the public address announcer saying, 'Gophers score. Rebound Gophers,' and so on. Finally, Bill turned around and asked, 'Who's this man, Gopher?' We never let him forget that!"

Bill didn't limit his collegiate athletic prowess solely to the basketball court. He ran track for IU, and he was a key runner when the track team won the Big Ten Track Championship. His personal records impressed fans and sports analysts alike. For example, he placed in the 220-yard Hurdles at the 1950 NCAA finals, and many observers considered him a likely candidate for the 1952 U.S. Olympic Team.

A careful review of *The Indiana Daily Student* newspapers from 1948-1951 provides an extremely accurate, chronological account of Bill's career at IU. While statistics tell one story, commentary and tone tell another. The first is simply a numerical account of a consummate athletic career, but the second is clearly the story of a beloved fellow student. Credits just don't get any better than that.

In sum, Indiana University's initiative changed the complexion of college basketball for all time. A deliberate choice of words, this statement reflects the course of events when Bill entered Indiana University. However, Bill's hometown also earned itself a special place in his success.

Shelbyville fans took credit — and legitimately so — for the small town where schools welcomed Negro children into competitive elementary and high school sports with no hint of discrimination. Those who delved into Bill's background came to a basic truth. A great deal of Bill Garrett's persona came from his upbringing and the wholesome atmosphere in which he was reared.

Ron Newlin, former Director of the Indiana Basketball Hall of Fame: "Had anyone in those years wanted to begin to rehabilitate Indiana race relations by recruiting the candidate with the perfect blend of skill and quiet confidence to break the color barrier in the Big Ten and to win the hearts of an entire state, they could have picked no better candidate than Shelbyville's Bill Garrett."

Accolades continued to amass in the media when Bill graduated from Indiana University, and his hometown was singularly proud of his great accomplishments. Bill's gentle character, molded from a combination of exemplary parental upbringing and even-handed, unbiased societal exposure, served him well during his college years.

Those who knew him best realized that, in sum, his childhood more than prepared him to handle the unrelenting mistreatment that he experienced at the college level — deliberately willful mistreatment which might have easily defeated a man with less inner strength. In the end, Bill, drawing on his inner strengths, not only ignored the undeserved mistreatment inflicted on him, but he also triumphed over it.

Chapter Eleven

B ill Garrett's college basketball career not only showcased his talent to regional fans, but it also piqued nationwide interest from professional basketball. When Bill graduated from IU with a Bachelor's Degree in Physical Education and a Minor in Business Administration, Boston Celtic officials chose him as the team's #3 draft pick. Bill failed to sign, but his decision had nothing at all to do with basketball. Another draft intervened — an altogether different kind of draft for a decidedly different team. Quite simply, it was an offer he couldn't refuse.

Just like the Celtics, "Uncle Sam" had draft plans in mind for IU star, Bill Garrett. As a result, instead of commencing on an exciting, challenging career in professional basketball, the fresh IU graduate reported for service with the United States Army in September of 1951.

After his first year in the Army, Bill and Betty made plans for their wedding. On August 2, 1952, the couple married in the Broadway Baptist Church, Madison, Indiana. Among the guests were four people with intensely personal ties to Bill's success as an IU basketball player. Two older couples sat proudly in the pews that night. Alongside Bill and Betty's childhood friends and college classmates, Branch and Mary Lou McCracken and Nate and Horte Kaufman witnessed the ceremony.

The wedding party included a best man, four grooms-men, five bridesmaids, and a matron of honor. Dr. James Roberson of Rochester, N.Y., Bill's college roommate, served as the best man, and Betty's older sister, Elinor Rhinehart, served as her Matron of Honor. Photos captured a truly stunning couple in the backseat of the car outside the church. Later, the newlyweds left for a two-week honeymoon at a resort in Niles, Michigan.

Because Bill was stationed at Fort Leonard Wood, Missouri, Betty sought a teaching position within a reasonable distance from his post. After a thorough search, she accepted a job at a Negro college in Pine Bluff, Arkansas. In spite of a busy work schedule, Betty managed to travel to Missouri to see Bill on weekends. Most trips were uneventful, however, one particular trip proved to be an extremely harrowing experience.

As Betty sat quietly on the bus, several white roughnecks began to harass her. She paid no heed to them, but they were not to be denied. In a short time, their crude actions and foul language increased to the point where she felt truly at risk for injury.

Somehow, she held out the hope that the driver would stop them, but instead of interceding on her behalf, the bus driver completely ignored the men's loud, unwelcome advances. The rascals took the driver's inaction as an open invitation to continue their cruel taunts. With no hint of punishment or consequences, their body language sent a clear message — they felt free to do whatever they wished. What began as a joyous sojourn for Betty had quickly developed into a trip of unbridled terror.

Betty trembled in fear — utterly helpless to ward off the men who hovered on every side. She didn't know exactly how far the men would go, but she was sure that nobody would raise a hand to stop them. She cringed as the possible outcomes flashed frantically through her mind.

The men grinned maliciously. Their evil expressions struck terror into the young woman. However, the culprits misjudged the passengers as individuals. A few rows down the aisle, a fellow traveler leaned out into the walkway and carefully assessed the barbaric behavior occurring a few yards away. He simply could not sit by and allow the men's actions to escalate any further. In a matter of seconds, he took action.

Silently, and stealthily, the uniformed man rose from his seat, towering to his full height. His head nearly brushed the ceiling of the bus. With an air of confidence and authority, the soldier strode down the aisle and met the group of hoodlums head-on.

To Betty's surprise, a situation that had rapidly spiraled out of control, came to a sudden, unexpected halt. The soldier shoved his way past the thugs, smiled wryly at them, and then slid into the seat beside the trembling young woman. Shocked and relieved, Betty slumped back into her seat.

Moments later, she leaned her face against the window and thanked God for what she considered an angel's intercession on her behalf. The remainder of the trip was uneventful, and the mood in the bus was far different when Betty alit from the gleaming metal steps at her final destination.

Time dragged for Bill and Betty that first year of their marriage. For them the lifestyle was excruciating. The devoted pair anguished over the pain of their forced separation. Betty busied herself at work. Meanwhile, scrimmage basketball games at the post passed the time for Bill. However, even rigorous competition failed to take the edge off the ache he felt for his wife.

Military service forestalled their foremost wish, a home together. Bill had no idea where he would serve, or how long he would serve, so he and Betty accepted their situation on its face. What neither one of them knew at the time was that Missouri would be the closest billet Bill would have for a long time. When orders came, they mandated overseas duty.

Bill suddenly found himself ordered to Korea. Betty remained in Pine Bluff and worked hard in two capacities, as a teacher and as the women's basketball coach. She shared her life with her soldier husband by mail — just as thousands of American women had done in past conflicts. Once she fulfilled her contract in Arkansas, Betty enrolled in Indiana University's Graduate School, where she earned a Master's Degree in Physical Education. Once more, she emerged from her Alma Mater as a new graduate looking for a job.

After researching available openings, Betty accepted a coaching position in a Toledo, Ohio, YWCA. At that time, Bill was still stationed in Korea, where he played basketball for the Army in a special sports unit. While playing for the US Army, Bill led his service team to a major championship. By the time he was discharged after 23 months of service on August 8, 1953, any hopes he held out for playing professional basketball had completely evaporated.

Because of his draft status, he lost his once-in-a-lifetime opportunity to play for The Celtics. Bill's age and the fact that he hadn't played competitively in the United States for over two years rendered him a poor choice for the draft. Major franchise scouts considered him too old to play professional basketball.

In the wake of such a bitter disappointment, Bill signed with the Harlem Globetrotters. Founded by Abe Saperstein in 1927, the Globetrotter organization occupied a special spot in the sports world.

Saperstein's teams maintained a solid reputation for both skill and comedic horseplay on the basketball court. From continent to continent, his talented athletes entertained millions of fans with a unique, fast-paced game, noted for levity. In the process, their polished antics polarized their two target groups. Rowdy clowning around humiliated their opponents and delighted their fans. As a result, the squad took pure basketball to new heights of finesse and artistry — all in the name of entertainment.

Despite the fact that the Saperstein's team played a distinctively different type of basketball, Bill took the job. As a new Globetrotter, he joined the ranks of legendary "Goose" Tatum and Marques Haynes, members of the Globetrotter team that defeated the World Champion Minneapolis Lakers in both 1948 and 1949.[27]

By the time Bill joined the Globetrotter roster in September of 1953, the franchise was considered the most competitive basketball organization in the nation. On worldwide tours, the team introduced the sport to people who had never seen a basketball before. Those trips earned them yet another name, "America's Ambassadors of Goodwill."[28]

Saperstein valued Bill Garrett. A Trotter press release cited the owner's opinion of his new player: "...with his ability and earnestness, (he) just can't miss."

If he could have played for any organization, the Globetrotters certainly — to put it facetiously — "fit the Bill." Their warm rapport with their worldwide audiences echoed an equal harmony that Bill shared with his college fans while he played for Indiana University.

Ultimately, Bill Garrett played a little more than two years for the world-renowned sports franchise. The "Trotters" intense, international schedule took him throughout Europe and South America. Most players found the cosmopolitan exposure an interesting and educational combination. To his credit, Bill tried to take the same view; yet, in the end, he deemed the nomadic lifestyle as exemplary, but lonely. He loathed living out of a suitcase and the constant travel. No doubt, he felt that way because he had been tens of thousands of miles away from Betty for so long while he was in the service. The constant foreign travel only intensified his burning desire to settle down in to a more ordered life. Quite simply, he wanted his wife. At the heart of it, Bill was a committed family man from the moment he said, "I do."

For the first time in his life, Bill quit playing basketball. In January of 1955, Bill left the Globetrotters. Just hours later, he arrived in Ohio to look for work. He landed a job doing piecework in a factory where management mandated a daily quota for men "on the line." Instead of judging his job as a series of mundane, boring repetitions, Bill viewed it as a personal challenge. His supervisors soon witnessed Bill surpass his assigned daily quota on a regular basis. His competitive nature kicked in with zest — probably to the dismay of his fellow workers, who just did just enough work to "get by."

While in the Toledo area, although Bill kept busy working in several area factories and foundries, he constantly monitored the job market in Hoosier high schools. In time, a suitable job surfaced. Both Betty and Bill were ecstatic to be "going home." In short order, both of them gave proper notice to their employers. Buoyed by Bill's job opportunity, and the added news that they were expecting their first child, two very happy people packed their belongings and moved back to Indiana.

Chapter Twelve

In 1956, The Indianapolis Public School System included a number of fine secondary schools. Among them was Harry E. Wood High School, located just a few blocks from Monument Circle, the commercial and physical hub of the state capital. In September, 1956, two Garretts joined the Wood faculty — Bill as a business teacher and basketball coach, and Betty as a physical education teacher.

The job at Wood suited Bill's needs. At that time, Indiana's coaching positions for Negroes were few and far between. Entry into the basketball program at Wood was a good "first step" on the ladder for him. Not only was he back in familiar surroundings, but he was also perfectly positioned to show what he could do as a high school coach in the capital city of a state renowned for highly competitive, crowd-pleasing basketball.

Crispus Attucks High School, a veritable powerhouse of Hoosier basketball, sat a short distance northwest of Wood High School. Unexpectedly, in 1957, Attucks veteran coach, Ray Crowe, decided to retire from his head coaching position and accept the job of Athletic Director. His decision proved pivotal to two lives.

Crispus Attucks retained a long-standing, excellent reputation, both academically and athletically. Its level of student achievement was widely acclaimed in Indiana educational circles. Key to this level of performance was the school's staff.

The school took its name for one of the three men killed instantly by the British soldiers in the Boston Massacre on March 3, 1770. Indianapolis' groundbreaking Negro high school boasted a faculty that included more instructors with Doctoral Degrees than any other high school in the state.

Taking the name of a Revolutionary War hero and martyr constituted a subtle message. Not only did the new school usher in a new phase of Negro public education, but it proclaimed a solid mission statement — to turn out first class American citizens, citizens worthy of Crispus Attucks' reputation.

Mathias Nolcox, the first principal of Crispus Attucks High School, assembled a teaching staff of Negro professionals from around the country long before the school opened in 1927. Although Negro students were scattered among the existing high school populations in the 1920s, Indianapolis Ku Klux Klan members wielded power in the offices of the mayor and the city council. That power not only alarmed the Negro community, but it also set the stage for racial division in the state capital — a division which may not have come about under other circumstances.

Nolcox hired many of his new teachers from Negro colleges in the South, and, over the summer the staff prepared for an incoming group of 1,000 students. Much to their surprise, administrators had grossly underestimated the enrollment, missing it by 350 students. Therefore, faculty increased at the beginning of the second year of the school's operation. Such exponential growth continued, unabated, and at no time during its operation as a fully segregated high school, did Attucks have adequate room for all its students and staff.

In addition, its evening division offered diplomas to hundreds of local Negroes who had never had an opportunity to earn a high school education. The building's interior blazed day and night, lighting the way for generations of Indianapolis people of all ages. The outstanding group of educators brought the school and its graduates wide acclaim, but the accolades were a mixture of both pain and pleasure. In fact, Attucks' success was a reflection of all levels of American education at that time.

Administrators assembled some of the brightest and most innovative Negro teachers in the nation, but many of those hired took jobs at the new high school because the majority of institutions of higher learning were closed to them.

Locally, the Indianapolis school system sorely limited opportunities for its own Negro educators. That situation, instead of being a bane to local Negro youth, actually became a boon. The shortage of Negro teachers drew an incredible group of educators to the Crispus Attucks High School students. Their teachers were "the cream of the crop."

When Attucks administrators announced the opening for Head Basketball Coach, they incited a professional frenzy. Scores of coaches saw it as the "plum" job in Indiana high school athletics. Bill Garrett applied for it immediately. In a short time, applications literally piled onto the desks of the screening committee. Considering Bill Garrett's credentials, those in charge of the search expected to find his application among the many candidates who submitted their resumes.

Further, in view of the small pool of available, qualified, experienced, Negro coaches, the Attucks fans were not the least bit surprised when the committee announced Garrett as its first choice. Bill joyously accepted the position. Many of the area coaches considered the head coaching job at Attucks to be "the job of a lifetime," and, deep inside, Bill, too, felt that statement held true. He knew how fortunate he was to have been selected. It was an unprecedented opportunity for someone his age. After all, he was just twenty-nine years old.

Bill saw his new job as Head Coach of The Crispus Attucks Tigers as a tremendous challenge. From the fans' perspective, their hopes ran high for the young coach, even though they knew he was still a bit green. On his side of the equation, Bill understood that he had been given a very big set of shoes to fill. Ray Crowe's coaching skills were impressive, and his reputation was sage.

According to Betty, a number of individuals claimed credit for Bill's selection as Crowe's replacement. However, Bill, in his laid-back manner, said very little in response to the persistent queries constantly hurled at him by a collection of people, including members of the press, his high school coaching peers, and a wide range of Attucks alumni.

People inside and outside of the Attucks community expected great things from Bill Garrett. Some of them even declared that they put a lot of pressure on the young coach. Bill never acknowledged those comments, but he possessed a balanced opinion of his own ability. His thoughts were both short and sweet. His classic response to the talk that swirled among the self-presumed movers and shakers of the time was delivered in a staid, calm voice. Replied Head Tigers Basketball Coach, Bill Garrett, "The only person who can put pressure on you is yourself."

In addition to his rigorous coaching schedule, Bill taught business classes at Attucks. He relished the classroom and enjoyed bonding with his students. Those on staff with Bill saw joy bubble within a very quiet man whenever he interacted with the young people in his care. Some of the most edifying comments about Bill, the teacher, came from a teaching peer of the time. His thoughts painted the portrait of a very complex and kind teacher.

A long-time Attucks instructor, he saw Bill as a man who loved to work with young people. According to him, " 'Mr. Garrett, the business teacher,' consistently stressed the importance of the need for a basic knowledge of business to his students. He understood that their adult lives would revolve around good management practices, both at work and at home."

In parallel, basketball offered the young coach an exceptionally attractive arena in which to work with young men — an arena not bounded by purely academic pressures, but an arena in which they could work hard and have fun.

First school for Shelbyville's Negro children (1869)

Teachers: Mr. Lewis R. Lewis and Miss Rose E. Dent (1903)

Reverend Robert D. Leonard, Minister Second Baptist Church, Shelbyville, Indiana (1903)

Congregation, Second Baptist Church, Shelbyville, Indiana (1903)

William L. Garrett, Winner, Shelby County Marble
Championship (1939)

Booker T. Washington School, Shelbyville, Indiana, no date
specified.

South Central Conference High School Track Meet: Bill Garrett wins, third lane from the left. (1946)

Bill Garrett cutting down the net after the Golden Bears won the Indiana State High School Basketball Championship, Butler Fieldhouse, Indianapolis, Indiana. (1947)

1947 Team Photo, 1947 State Champions, TheShelbyville Golden Bears - Row 1: Louis Bower, Everett Burwell, Bill Breck, Emerson Johnson, Don Robinson. Row 2 - Asst. Coach Arthur "Doc" Barnett, Marshall Murray, Don Chambers, Bill Breedlove, Bill Garrett, Loren "Hank" Hemingway, Head Coach Frank Barnes. Courtesy, IHSAA and Tiffany Studios, Broad Ripple.

Triumphant Golden Bears riding atop the Ariens Fox Pumper hours after winning the State Championship. *The Shelbyville Democrat*. Bill Garrett back row, third from left. Note the top coats and hats! (1947)

Aerial view of Shelbyville High School campus.

Bonfire at The Shelby County Courthouse on the night The Golden Bears won the State Title. (1947)

William Leon Garrett, Shelbyville High School Class of 1947

"Their First Coach" – State Champions, from left to right, Bill Garrett, Emerson "Emmie" Johnson, and Marshall Murray with Dr. Walter Stanton Fort. Dr. Fort holds the 1947 Indiana State High School Basketball Championship Trophy. *The Shelbyville Democrat*, 1947.

Shelbyville High School Baseball Team, Bill Garrett, Row 3, third from left. (1947)

Indiana's 1947 High School Basketball All Stars, Bill Garrett, fourth from right and Phil Buck, Captain, fifth from right. (1947)

Indiana's Bill Garrett, Number 8 (1948)
Courtesy of Indiana University Archives.

Indiana University President, Herman B Wells
Courtesy of Indiana University Archives.

The 1949-50 "Hurryin' Hoosiers," Bill Garrett, Row 1, third from right. Courtesy of Indiana University Archives.

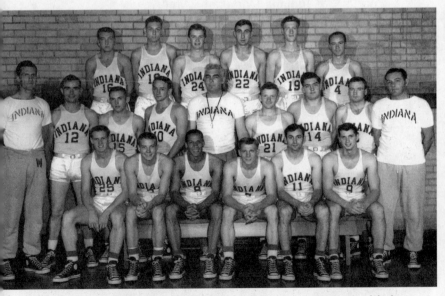

The 1950-51 "Hurryin' Hoosiers," Bill Garrett, Row 1, third from left. Courtesy of Indiana University Archives.

Indiana Head Basketball Coach, Branch McCracken holding
a clinic in The Indiana University Fieldhouse, Bill Garrett,
on the floor, third from right (first player nearly obscured).
Courtesy of Indiana University Archives.

Interior View, Indiana University Fieldhouse
Courtesy of Indiana University Archives.

February 27, 1950, Indiana vs. Illinois: Bill Garrett (#8) with a lay-up for the Hoosiers.
Courtesy of Indiana University Archives.

Bill Garrett, Indiana University Track Star at Memorial
Stadium, June 1, 1950.
Courtesy of Indiana University Archives.

Bill Garrett accepting trophy for Outstanding Senior Athlete,
Indiana University, Spring, 1951.
Courtesy of Indiana University Archives.

Bill Garrett and Indiana Head Coach, Branch McCracken
No year specified.
Courtesy of Indiana University Archives.

United States Army Basketball Squad, Fort Leonard Wood,
Missouri. (1952)
Courtesy of Betty Garrett Inskeep.

"Together — at last!"
William Leon and Betty Guess Garrett
August 2, 1952, Madison, Indiana.
Courtesy of Betty Garrett Inskeep.

"Sweet Georgia Brown!" Bill as a Harlem Globetrotter 1953
Courtesy of Harlem Globetrotters, Phoenix, Arizona, Govoner
Vaughn, Archivist.

"Off and Running!" Bill Garrett as Assistant Varsity Track Coach, Crispus Attucks High School, Row 2, far right. (1959) *The Tiger*, 1959 (Crispus Attucks High School Yearbook).

"Back Home Again!" February 20, 1959: The Crispus Attucks Tigers play The Shelbyville Golden Bears for the first time in a regular season at The Paul Cross Gym. L-R: Frank Barnes, SHS Athletic Director (Bill's Coach for the 1947 State Championship), Golden Bears Head Coach Leroy "Dee" Compton, and Bill Garrett, Head Coach of the Tigers. Picture taken in front of the trophy case. Note the picture of the '47 team in the background.

"Bench Anxiety!" 1959 State Tournament Season. Left, Assistant Coach Don Thomas and Head Coach Bill Garrett. *The Tiger*, 1959 (Crispus Attucks High School Yearbook).

Tiger Cheerleaders, 1959. L-R: Jane Coleman, Cynthia Ford, Regenia Bridgeforth, and Mary Smith. *The Tiger*, 1959.

"Victory!" Coach Bill Garrett on the shoulders of his 1959 State Champion Tigers. Butler Fieldhouse, March, 1959. No source cited.

1959 Indiana State High School Basketball Champions! The Crispus Attucks Tigers with Coaches Don Thomas (Back Row, far right) and Bill Garrett (Back Row, fourth from right). Butler Fieldhouse, Indianapolis, Indiana.

"Time to swim!" Bill with Billy. (1970)

MEMORIAL SERVICE

FOR

Mr. William "Bill" Garrett

SATURDAY, AUGUST 10, 1974

11:00 A. M.

WITHERSPOON UNITED PRESBYTERIAN CHURCH
Indianapolis, Indiana

REV. LANDRUM E. SHIELDS, PASTOR

ACTIVE PALLBEARERS

Elders of Witherspoon United Presbyterian Church

Clarence Wood

E. Paul Thomas

Rozelle Boyd

Eugene Taylor

Edward Bond

Nicky Morris

HONORARY PALLBEARERS

Clifton Anderson

James Ballow

Dijvan Boyd

Richard Boyd

William Bradley

Harold Brown

Henry Bundles

Alvin Bynum

Jerry Center

John Coleman

Julian Coleman

Ray Crowe

George DeCoursey

William DesPres

James Doyle

Reginald DuValle

Russel Freeland

Charles Guess

William Guess

Ferdinand Hardy

George Hight

Frank Holloway

John Jenkins

Clarence Johnson

Emerson Johnson

Frank Johnson

Robert Jones

Bart Kaufman

Nate Kaufman

Robert La Rue

Frank Lloyd

William Malone

Ezzell Marrs

Graham Martin

Gordon Mickey

Alexander Moore

Chester Mullins

Lincoln Murphy

Marshall Murray

Harry Pettrie

Don Phillips

James Pipes

Gerald Preusz

James Robeson

William Scott

Robert Smith

Seab Stowers

Joseph Stuart

George Taliaferro

Don Thomas

Leroy Vertner

Mike Wagoner

Marshall Ware

Waterford Lodge No. 13

John White

John Wicks

Johnny Wilson

Hugh Wolf

ORDER OF SERVICE

PROCESSIONAL . . . . Soft Music

ENTRANCE OF FAMILY

PRAYER

ANTHEM—"Let There Be Peace" . . . . . . Westminsteraires

SCRIPTURE READING . . . . Psalm 90

THE FAMILY EULOGY . . . . Elder William Malone

SOLO—"Lord's Prayer . . . . Mr. Jack Romby

WORDS OF COMFORT . . . . Rev. Landrum E. Shields

BENEDICTION

RECESSIONAL

COMMITTAL

INTERMENT . . . . Crown Hill Cemetery

* * * * * *

APPRECIATION

ON BEHALF OF THE FAMILY, WE WISH TO EXPRESS THEIR
GRATITUDE FOR YOUR MANY KINDNESSES, AS EVIDENC-
ED IN THOUGHT AND DEED, AND FOR YOUR ATTENDING
THIS MEMORIAL SERVICE.

STUART MORTUARY, INC.

Chapter Thirteen

A s a result of his philosophy, Bill Garrett capitalized on every moment he spent coaching his players. Although there is no concrete evidence that any one teacher or coach influenced Bill's decision to pursue a career in high school education and athletics, the quality of his own high school teachers must be highlighted. In the 1930s and 1940s, some of the most respected and highly paid individuals were public school teachers. Their imprint on Bill's life is indelible.

J. M. "Mac" McKeand, Arthur "Doc" Barnett, Ruth Keith, Esther Kinsley, Deloris McDonald, Georgia Moore, and Lawrence "Boots" Thompson were just a few of those educators who made up the faculty of Shelbyville High School. Bill Garrett took a serious approach to teaching—an approach that harkened back to his days as a high school student. What's more, he drew on his two varsity basketball coaches when he began his own coaching career.

The crux of the matter was that coaching basketball provided Bill Garrett a very attractive connection to the younger generation. He not only taught the fundamentals of the game, but he also set an excellent, personal example for those in his charge. His temperament, his level of dedication, his relentless pursuit of excellence, and his personality all blended together to make him an unrivaled role model for the rapidly maturing high school players who soon hung on his every word.

As he began to spend time with his Attucks basketball players, Coach Garrett guided them. Even more, he inspired them — not only to hone and polish their athletic skills, but also to aspire to be fine men. It didn't take long for Tiger basketball fans to realize that their new coach was a capable replacement for his legendary predecessor.

At home, just as at school, Bill's life changed and his personal responsibilities increased. The Garrett family grew quickly. Within three years after they moved to Indianapolis, Bill and Betty had three daughters, Tina, Judy, and Laurie.

Bill and Betty rejoiced in their children. They finally had the family they had always wanted. In the meantime, on the athletic front, Bill's basketball team improved at a fast clip. Pundits judged the 1958-59 season ripe for success. To many Attucks fans, their Tigers looked like excellent contenders for the state tournament.

IU teammates Phil Buck and Bill Garrett both coached high school basketball — Bill at Crispus Attucks and Phil at Anderson Madison Heights. One day, Buck called his Hurryin' Hoosier pal and invited him to come to Anderson to see a new offense in action. Intrigued, Bill drove over and watched the offense in person.

During the scrimmage game, Bill studied every move on the floor with great intensity. He asked question after question, probing the fine points of maneuvers executed by the Madison Heights Pirates. Heartened and encouraged by what he had seen, Bill thanked his friend and returned home.

In March, Bill coached the Crispus Attucks Tigers to the State Championship in Butler Fieldhouse — the same arena in which he had played for the 1947 Shelbyville Golden Bears. That fateful night in 1959, Coach Bill Garrett joined the ranks of an elite group in Hoosier high school basketball history — those few men who achieved the Indiana High School Championship as both a player and a coach.

More specifically, Bill wrote a new page of Hoosier sports history when his Attucks Tigers won that final game in 1959. That night, Bill Garrett became the only man in Indiana basketball history to win the title of Indiana's "Mr. Basketball" as a youngster and go on, in later life, to coach his own team to the coveted title of Indiana High School State Basketball Champions.

In Buck's words, "I can't be sure, of course, but I like to think that I had a little something to do with Bill's success in the 1959 State Tournament. I think he used that new offense to good advantage during his tournament games."

Bill maintained close contact with his former Hoosier teammates, especially those closest to him. The men shared a close bond for each other and, in addition, they all had a soft spot in their hearts for Coach McCracken's wife. For many years, former IU basketball players — to a man — considered Mary Jo McCracken as a second mother.

When former West Point Coach, Robert Montgomery Knight, was selected as Branch McCracken's replacement at Indiana University, Mary Jo called Bill Garrett and Phil Buck. Although she knew there had been no formal announcement of Knight's selection, she decided to invite some of her husband's former players to come to her home to meet Bob Knight in person. Also in attendance that evening were Charlie Meyer and Tony Hill.[29]

The men had an amiable visit with the new coach, and they tried to give him a little insight on the history of Indiana basketball. More specifically, the group stressed the personal importance of the close relationships IU players shared long after they graduated and had gone their separate ways. Many of the players who talked with Knight that evening were current Indiana high school basketball coaches, men who valued their experiences at Indiana and the lasting friendships formed while students in Bloomington. Bill was a good example of that kind of player.

Bill really appreciated his education, and he used it to good advantage. That, of course, also applied to his athletic abilities. Even though he had a full-time job as Attucks Head Basketball Coach, he didn't limit himself to that sport alone.

In the basketball off-season, he served as Assistant Track Coach. Coupled with teaching business and taking an active part in his children's lives, Bill Garrett was a very busy individual.

Like Bill, Betty also balanced two careers. In addition to coaching and teaching at Wood High School, she reared three, very active, little girls. She credited her success as a dual effort, citing the fact that she had wonderful help in her home. When she left for school each morning, the girls were in the experienced, capable hands of an excellent babysitter who came to the Garrett home weekdays.

In Betty's words, "Bobbie Hardy was a remarkable woman. A mother of six, she took over those children and did beautifully. She was dependable, reliable, and loving — in essence, what anyone would want in a babysitter. I was so busy then. I remember that many people asked me what I did. Their questions baffled me. To be truthful, it was all I could do to get through my day and go home and get our girls ready to go to the gym. A lot of times, we arrived just a few minutes before the tip-off at a home game."

Already accustomed to a hectic teaching schedule, Betty found motherhood fraught with very daunting challenges, if only in terms of time management. In a matter of a few years, the girls' extra-curricular activities put even more strain on their mother's busy schedule. The entire family loved athletics, but the girls fell in love with one sport in particular, and their choice awakened Betty's memories of growing up in a small, picturesque, Southern Indiana town.

Betty's childhood experiences in Madison, Indiana, not only shaped her attitude about social boundaries, but they also propelled her into a lifelong profession. Madison's public swimming pool barred "children of color." With the only safe swimming venue closed to them, the Negro children of Jefferson County, Indiana, were forced to learn to swim elsewhere.

As a direct result of that racial bias, many children drowned—not only in the unpredictable currents of the mighty Ohio River — but also in a number of the smaller steams that spilled into the busy waterway separating Indiana from neighboring Kentucky.

The memory of those needless deaths made a deep impression on Betty, and, in turn, predicted her future. As a high school student, she vowed to become a swimming coach. She not only wanted to teach Negro children to swim in safety, but she also wanted to coach them to swim in competition.

Betty recognized the value of competitive athletics to children. From personal experience, she knew that athletics instilled good moral values and built self-esteem. Once she saw the spark of competition light a fire in her own little girls, she expected them to be able to compete on an equal basis against anyone in the city. Unfortunately, much to Betty's surprise and shock, the stigma of race threatened to completely derail the girls' hopes of swimming in open competition.

A devoted mother, Betty did her best to set a strong example for her girls, especially when it came to showing the grit and determination required for them to succeed in life. Because she knew that inner strength played a big part in athletic competition, she was determined to find the girls a swim club. Her heart ached for the little girls, and she didn't want them to feel unwanted or unworthy.

The unfair attitudes and practices she and Bill encountered as children should have changed by the time they reared their girls. Alas, this was not the case at all, for racial progress, if there had been any, was almost imperceptible. Betty combed the area in search of a suitable swim club for her girls, but, despite her dogged efforts, she could not convince a single Indianapolis facility to accept the three girls on a swim team. After weeks of searching, she failed to find one manager who was willing to enroll her girls.

Frustrated at the rebuffs to his wife's pleas, Bill took on the search as a personal challenge. Bill never acted as if he deserved any special personal or professional consideration when faced with a difficult job. Humility was his hallmark. Even with his established identity and high profile in Indiana sports, he was not the kind of man who ever "threw his weight around."

In fact, to all who knew him, he lived his life as if he were no better or worse than anyone else. His modus operandi was working with people, one on one, and eye to eye.

A self-confident man, Bill worked in a very quiet way. After much consideration, he approached this particular quest just as he had all the other problems he had encountered in his life — with zest. Because he didn't anticipate a great deal of difficulty in securing a place for his girls to swim, he began with the best known, most high profile facilities.

First, he contacted the officials at The Jordan "Y." They refused. Disappointed, and a bit surprised, he continued his search. Finally, after many attempts, Bill succeeded. Bill DesPres, Swimming Coach of The Krannert "Y," graciously accepted the girls into his program. This was a "first" for Krannert, and for the Negro community.

Because of DesPres' progressive thinking, Tina, Judy, and

Laurie Garrett swam on the Krannert team for years, and, in the process, won a string of impressive ribbons and trophies. For the record, the Garrett family was the first Negro family to swim competitively in the city of Indianapolis. Once again, the name Garrett was synonymous with pacesetting change in athletics.

High standards were core to the Garrett household, and it was clear that all three girls benefited from their parents' wholesome values. Reflecting their own upbringing, Bill and Betty's strong Christian faith provided their girls a stable influence in their lives from the time they were born.

The entire family actively participated in The Witherspoon Presbyterian Church. Bill served as an elder, and Betty taught junior high Sunday school. The children grew up with a religious background that stressed the importance of values and morals and the security derived from a loving, caring home.

As the girls grew older, school obligations and activities increased. In time, each of the girls had individual interests, and each new interest drastically altered the entire family's schedule. However, the busy household was destined for even more excitement.

In December of 1964, a fourth child arrived. Named for both his father and mother, William Guess Garrett was quickly dubbed "Billy." Betty continued to teach, and assumed her new responsibility with characteristic poise. The word "busy" didn't come close to describing the frenetic activity of the Garrett household in the mid-1960s. The girls helped out with their little brother, and, with all four children in tow, Betty marshaled her troops to the Attucks home basketball games on a regular basis.

Bill stressed a sense of balance to each of his children. He consistently instilled a keen sense of responsibility in his daughters, both in terms of academics and athletics. They knew what was expected of them, and they worked hard to achieve those goals.

As he continued to teach and coach at Attucks, Bill enrolled at Butler University, from which he earned both a Master's Degree in Education and a Guidance Certificate in 1968. Inside, Bill wanted another challenge. It was time for a change.

In 1969, after ten years as Head Coach of the Crispus Attucks Tigers, Bill stepped aside and took the job of Athletic Director, a position he held for two years. During his work in that position, he reconnected with an old friend.

Bill's IU teammate, Phil Buck, coached a high school basketball team several counties away from Indianapolis. While Bill was "A.D." at Attucks, he and Buck scheduled Anderson Madison Heights to play Crispus Attucks during the regular season. This was a bold move for Buck, but the games went off flawlessly, with no problems whatsoever. It was the first time Bill and Phil had worked together at the high school level since they were named to 1947 Indiana All Stars, a team on which Bill played and Phil was Captain.

The old friends gained a lot of satisfaction from the opportunity to work together, and they took a lot of pride in seeing their two teams move into a wider, more racially diverse, arena of high school athletic competition.

Chapter Fourteen

The next step in Bill's professional educational career came at the collegiate level. In 1971, he accepted a job as Director of Continuing Education at Indiana Vocational Technical College. Today, most Indianapolis residents know the institution simply by the name, "IVY Tech."

College administration came naturally to Bill, and he enjoyed his job very much. Vocational training in the Indianapolis area was sorely limited for high school graduates. For that reason alone, IVTC filled a very important slot on the Indianapolis education menu. It is important to note, however, that Indianapolis had a long history of providing vocational education at the high school level.

After the Civil War, Indianapolis schools followed the national trend and integrated manual training into their curricula. The Indianapolis Industrial Training School opened in 1895. Later, its name was changed to Emmerich Manual Training High School, or for short, "Manual." In 1904, Arsenal Technical High School opened on the site of a US Army Arsenal just east of downtown. Nicknamed "Tech" by local residents, its land deed included a caveat mandating that any educational institution placed on the grounds be open to both boys and girls.

Over time, Tech expanded its vocational offerings to include graphic and commercial art, printing, and the building trades. Later, the school added classes in radio, automotive mechanics, and commerce.

During much the same time period, a number of private and charitable groups also joined in a concerted effort to train young people. In 1890, The Girls Industrial School of Indianapolis opened with 20 children. By 1907, enrollment stood at 736 and the facility offered classes in stenography, sewing, typewriting, and home economics. The Winona Agricultural and Technical Institute, another early private trade school, sat on the land later used by Arsenal Tech.[30]

Although local interest sparked the vocational training movement in Indianapolis, international events not only influenced the types of vocational training in Indiana, but across the nation as well. World War II prompted military offshoots in the courses offered by these schools. War-related offerings such as aeronautics, mapping, military drawing, and code training made their way into the Tech curriculum. Following the war, a surge of returning veterans prompted an even greater interest in post-secondary vocational training in Indianapolis.[31]

Harry E. Wood High School, opened in the fall of 1953, was built for the specific purpose of providing excellent vocational education to the city's young people.

At the time Bill took his job with IVTC, the school was a fledgling institution. During his tenure, enrollment increased from 6,386 to 7,415 students. Courses included certification in a number of disciplines in both the mechanical and clerical areas. He relished his new job, and he threw himself into school operations with great enthusiasm.

His efforts did not go unnoticed by others in the area, and, in a short time, he received another job offer — this time at a very familiar institution.

Administrators at Indiana University's Indianapolis campus noted Bill's considerable administrative talent with great interest. Spurred on by his accomplishments at IVTC, they asked him to accept a job on their staff. Indiana University-Purdue University-Indianapolis, like Wood and Attucks, sat close to the city center. Because of its inordinately long name, the institution went by the acronym, IUPUI. The search committee needed someone on staff to work with students at risk of dropping out of school. After much discussion, they considered Bill Garrett the ideal candidate.

Bill was thrilled by the offer, and he accepted it gladly. After seventeen years of teaching in the classroom, coaching on the basketball court, and advising adult students in a vocational school, Bill took on a challenging, administrative role on a major Indiana college campus.

In 1973, he began his new job as IUPUI's Assistant Dean of Student Activities. The rapidly expanding, urban campus sat alongside, and complemented, the grounds of the highly-respected Indiana University School of Medicine and its adjacent hospitals. Bill's new position at IUPUI not only offered him another opportunity to advise and guide young people at the college level, but it also led him back to his Alma Mater as a faculty member.

At IUPUI, Bill found himself on the front lines of a rapidly growing metropolitan university. His broad experience in education gave him a firm foundation for his new responsibilities. He adored his work and never shied away from difficult situations. He helped students through a variety of personal and academic challenges. A mentor of immense capabilities, Bill had finally found his niche.

Working with the students on the IUPUI campus gave Bill the chance to mentor in "one-on-one" situations. He had empathy for those who felt they were victims of discrimination, and he had sympathy for those who were trying desperately to find the right path for their lives. His years spent teaching and coaching, coupled with his experience as a father of four, girded him with both understanding and common sense.

Perhaps his listening skills served him best of all. His habit of talking little and listening much aided him in counseling his "at risk" students. He cared deeply about young people. He saw them as the future. Because students in his care recognized his sincerity at the outset, they responded to his suggestions. Suddenly, Bill's life blossomed in ways he had never anticipated.

Bill also served on an Indiana University Advisory Board during 1973. In addition, he ran for a seat on the Board of Trustees, losing by only a few votes to a Black faculty member on the Bloomington campus. Bill loved Indiana University. His loyalty to his Alma Mater never waned, and whenever Indiana University called on him to serve, he did so with energy and passion.

An extremely close couple, both Bill and Betty reveled in their marriage and took great pride in their children. Busy schedules, however, left little time for personal, adult celebrations. Weekends were earmarked for household chores and minor repairs, common to all homeowners with growing families.

By the middle of the summer of 1974, everything in Bill's life was moving along nicely. The girls were busy with their activities and looked forward to the start of school in a matter of weeks. Billy, then an active nine-year-old boy, played basketball at every opportunity. The household grew accustomed to hearing the sound of a ball bouncing in the driveway. Billy, like countless other Indianapolis nine-year-olds, aimed well, but many shots failed to go in the hoop. A broken pane in a garage window bore witness to one of his missed attempts.

The girls were rapidly becoming young women, and their

high school activities sparked the entire family. Feminine, breathless repartee was definitely part of every family meal. Nine-year-old Billy's antics amused and delighted his older sisters, as well as his parents. Both Bill and Betty basked in the joy of a growing, healthy family.

On Saturday morning, the day after their 32nd anniversary, Betty awoke early and went downstairs to make out a grocery list and devise her game plan for errands. For some unknown reason, she decided to go back upstairs and kiss Bill good-bye. He was barely awake when she went in the room. She leaned down and kissed him gently. Before she rose to leave the room, she whispered, "I love you. I'll see you later."

He replied, "I love you, too."

Sometime that day, Bill measured the broken window and backed out of the driveway. He headed for Zayre's, a large, local discount store. Once he arrived there, he went inside, where a hardware clerk cut a replacement pane. Minutes later, he stood in line for the cashier, patiently holding the piece of glass, carefully wrapped in brown paper.

Suddenly, Bill's knees buckled and he collapsed. For a few moments, people reeled in alarm, but nobody did anything. Luckily, a medical doctor waited in a nearby checkout lane. The doctor vaulted the checkout counter between them and rushed to Bill's aid. Quickly, he knelt by Bill's side and checked for vital signs. Bill's heart had stopped. Immediately, the physician ripped off Bill's shirt and began to administer CPR. At the same time, someone called an ambulance. Finally, the doctor felt a pulse.

Betty returned from her grocery shopping and errands in early afternoon. She was busy putting away her purchases when the doorbell rang. She walked from the kitchen to the front door and opened it. A policeman stood on the front porch.

Somehow, she knew that he brought bad news and, deep inside, she knew that the news was about Bill. She had no way of knowing, yet she sensed it the minute she looked at the officer's face.

He told her that Bill had been taken by ambulance to Methodist Hospital. The next hours were a blur of frantic calls, friends arriving at the hospital, and a series of doctors updating her on Bill's condition. Simultaneously, Methodist's Emergency Room personnel worked frantically to do whatever they could to save his life.

Doctors told Betty that Bill's brain had been deprived of oxygen for much too long. In fact, they did not expect him to regain consciousness. If he did survive, there was every possibility that he would be, for want of a better word, a "vegetable." Although Bill was never on any kind of life support, he lived for a time. Ever the fighter, he clung desperately to life. Yet, in the end, the damage was far too severe, and, four days later, Bill died.

Sports editors across the Midwest led with the headline of Bill's death. From Shelbyville and Indianapolis to Bloomington and Chicago, bold, black type reflected the mood of every sports fan with a grasp of collegiate basketball history.

While most journalists focused only on Bill's accomplishments, one did not. Instead, in his August 8, 1974, column distributed by The Chicago Tribune Press Service, David Condon quoted one of Bill's former college coaches " His track coach at IU, Frank Jones, said, 'He took a lot of working over when he arrived, but I never knew him to get mad.' 'Never knew him to get mad,' a pretty epitaph for a man who died too young."

Reeling in shock from the sudden loss, Betty turned to friends. Daisy Lloyd, Betty's obstetrician's wife, stepped in and took over all the necessary duties. She selected the casket, scheduled the wake, and made all the arrangements for the services, including the burial plot. First, the mortuary held calling hours in the afternoon. Then, The Witherspoon Presbyterian Church hosted an evening wake the night before the funeral. When church officials realized that the wake was drawing a huge crowd, they asked the police to control traffic along busy Michigan Road. A constant stream of cars caused gridlock on the busy thoroughfare for hours.

When Betty and the children arrived at the wake, Betty's closest friends were very concerned about her well being. They could see that the evening was bound to be very hard on the young widow. Enter Bill's close friend, IU football great, George Talliafero.

George drove up from Bloomington with his wife, Viola. When they walked in the door, Viola squired the children aside and looked after them for the rest of the evening. George stepped up to the casket and stood beside Betty for the entire wake. He never left her side. According to Betty, his acts of chivalry and compassion meant more to her than he could have imagined.

The line of mourners continued, unabated, for hours. Finally, the minister felt compelled to close the doors. He knew that there was just so much that the family could endure. Speaking softly, he encouraged those left outside to attend the services at the church the next morning.

Like the calling hours and the wake, the funeral drew an overflow crowd. Luminaries from high school, college, and professional basketball joined family, friends, fellow educators, former students and unnumbered others who just wanted to come and honor a real American hero. Although there was not a formal count, the crowd was estimated to be in the thousands.

Hetty Gray

That day, the sad, shocked faces of the pallbearers mirrored the loss felt throughout the entire state. Bill's hometown, intensely proud of his accomplishments, joined countless other communities throughout Indiana in mourning his loss. Stunned, Shelbyville grieved deeply for one of its own.

Characteristically, Bill Garrett's funeral was eloquent, "to the point," and brief. The service format precisely mirrored the tack that he took as he faced, and surmounted, the immense challenges over the course of his life. Bill's pastor and close friend, Reverend Landrum Shields, officiated. The funeral program, consisting of two songs and a short message, preceded final interment in the state capital's largest cemetery that lay just a few blocks south of the church.

Crown Hill Cemetery, the nation's third largest cemetery, derives its name from its highest point, 750 feet above the level of downtown. The entire area is a sylvan forest, lush with more than 250 species of trees and shrubs. Wildlife abounds within its confines. Listed on the National Register of Historic Places, the cemetery draws more than 25,000 visitors each year.[32] By day, the entire area delights the eyes of drivers on nearby streets. By night, it looms as a vast, dark square below planes that pass along the glide path to the local airport from north to south. The resting spot of countless loved ones, young and old, that warm August day — quite unexpectedly — Crown Hill lay to rest a beloved man.

Bill Garrett never thought of himself as a celebrity, but, in fact he was, and he joined many other famous Hoosiers at Crown Hill. The long list of notables buried there includes President Benjamin Harrison, Hoosier Poet James Whitcomb Riley, three former Vice-Presidents — Thomas A. Hendricks (another Shelbyville native), Charles W. Fairbanks, and Thomas Riley Marshall — ten Indiana governors, and fourteen Indianapolis mayors.[33]

Its namesake, the "Crown Hill," atop the sprawling interdenominational cemetery, commands the highest vantage point in the city. There, visitors look down from its heights onto a city that Bill Garrett loved, moreover, a city that loved Bill Garrett.

Among the mourners was Dr. James Roberson, Bill's college roommate, who traveled from New York State for Bill's services. A highly respected, successful Obstetrician-Gynecologist, "Robey" asked Betty and the children to come to his hotel room the day after the funeral. He wanted to talk about what had happened to his forty-five-year-old friend. He recalled that day as one of the hardest in his life.

Bill died from arrhythmia, a condition in which the heart fibrillated uncontrollably, and Robey did his best to explain to Betty how that pattern differed from the even rhythm of a normal heart. He told her that when Bill's heart began to fibrillate, it never relaxed. Unable to keep up the frenetic pace, his heart stopped

Much to Dr. Roberson's chagrin, he knew that his profession had its limitations. He tried his best to impress upon Betty that there were times when the doctors could do nothing. She nodded in agreement.

She remembered what the doctors told her at the hospital several days before. She knew that had Bill survived, he would have existed in a vegetative state. The doctors had been straightforward with her. She understood anatomy and physiology. Her physical education background gave her a good grasp of the crisis point in the whole tragedy — Bill's brain had been without oxygen for far too long before emergency personnel began to resuscitate him.

After spending time with Robey, she refused to give in to her grief. She had a job to do. She had four children. In classic response, Betty mustered her courage and launched herself into a role of a single parent. She held her family together and returned to teaching. The children girls attended Shortridge High School and Billy attended School 86. Her first goal was to see that life "returned to normal" as soon as possible, for all their sakes. Faced with rearing the children without a father, Betty steeled herself for the challenge. She had faced hard times before, and she had faith that she could weather this as well.

Word spread quickly about Bill's passing, yet some people didn't hear of his death until days, and sometimes, weeks later. One such person was IU teammate Phil Buck. He and his family were on vacation in Michigan when Bill died and they didn't learn of his death until they returned home to Indiana. Immediately upon hearing the news, Phil and his wife drove to Indianapolis to visit with Betty. The Bucks made a vow to keep in touch with Betty and support her in any way that they could.

Later, Phil carefully and consistently followed Billy's progress as he went through high school. Unlike his sisters, Billy attended Crispus Attucks, where he played on the basketball team. Schedule permitting, Phil took every opportunity to attend Attucks home games. One night in particular, he took his assistant with him. As a matter of fact, that night made quite an impression on Phil.

Lou Cotton, the Pirates' Assistant Coach, was Black. He accompanied Phil to the Attucks game that night. The junior varsity game had just ended, and there was the typical lull between the "JV" game and the varsity tip-off.

When Phil and Lou walked into the packed gymnasium, they noticed the assembled masses of people scrutinizing them. Phil was confident that Betty would be somewhere in the stands, so he began to walk up and down the edge of the court in front of the home crowd. He scanned the crowd for her face. In the end, she spotted him first.

To the Tiger crowd's surprise, Betty jumped to her feet, skipped down the eight rows of bleachers, and threw her arms around her old friend. Phil recalled the scene with his typical sense of humor.

"I can still see all those people watching us. I know they must have been saying to one another, 'What on earth is going on down there?'

"Well, Lou and I followed Betty back up in the stands and sat with her for the entire game. As word spread about our identities, scores of folks came down to sit and visit with us. It was a wonderful evening. I can't begin to say how many people I chatted with that night, but there were certainly a lot of them. One thing's for sure, so long as Billy lives, Bill lives. The young man looks so much like his father. It's just amazing to me just how much he looks like his father."

Chapter Fifteen

"His life was gentle; and the elements so mix'd in him that Nature might stand up and say to all the world, 'This was a man!'"

– William Shakespeare

Few men leave tangible evidence of their sojourn through this existence we call life. Some works survive their creators, such as the writings of the bard cited above, but, alas, that is the exception, not the rule. Closing this biography presents a solid opportunity to address the meaning of immortality — not in the Biblical sense, but in terms of legacy.

Indiana's love affair with basketball is one of legendary proportions. Hoosiers have "lived and died basketball" for well over a century. Indiana's "one class, winner take all, high school basketball tournament" enthralled homegrown fans and dazzled out-of-state observers. Of the major changes that took place over time, perhaps the most unsung was the smooth integration among the races in the smaller school districts. Shelbyville epitomized that change, because it brought Negroes and whites together at the seventh grade level years before administering total integration in all twelve grades.

The children of Shelbyville played together. They played in the streets and alleys. They played in the parks. They played on schoolyard ball diamonds and basketball courts. The children, reflecting the older generation, enjoyed one another. Overall, Shelbyville's residents got along beautifully.

The adults worked with one another, or for one another. The churches came together as a family and aided any one congregation in distress. The schools competed against one another. Although some lines of discrimination existed, those lines fell short of violence and insulated the Negro children from the travails of larger cities. Although limits were imposed, they were accepted for what they were, despite their unfairness.

This atmosphere fostered a calm, steady environment for growing children, no matter what their color or ethnicity. Christian and Jew, Negro and white, rich and poor — all people lived together in the haven of a small, rural community. To a large degree, and for its time, that environment sheltered its Negro children from the harsh rhetoric of the large cities...from the threat of harm at the hands of bigoted thugs...from the heartache caused by unwarranted and unreasonable hatred...from the ugly world of racism....

One of the many young people who had the opportunity grew up in such a place was William Leon Garrett, born April 4, 1929.

The child of a small, Indiana town, Bill Garrett strode through life as a participant, not as an observer. He competed with the skill of a gladiator, protected with the heart of a lion, and counseled with the tenderness of a loving father. Despite his sudden, untimely death, he left a legacy that never died.

This chapter is a litany of memories from those who knew him best. More than a recitation of words on paper, these testimonials are prayers of thanksgiving for a dear and valued friend.

Louis "Gene" Byrd – Member, Second Baptist Church; Garrett family friend:

"I watched Bill grow up. Like other members of the church, I took great pride in Bill's accomplishments. He was always a very quiet boy, but extremely polite. I remember him when he played in the county marble tournament. He took competition seriously, even at an early age. Later, my brother, Richard, and I followed Bill from high school through college. We went to IU with Bill's family on several occasions. When the athletic schedules allowed, we made a day of it. We drove down early and enjoyed the afternoon football game before going over to the IU Fieldhouse to watch Bill play in the evening. Our entire community was a family. To me, those were truly wonderful times."

Pauline Scott – Schoolmate; Shelbyville High School, 1948; Member, Second Baptist Church:

"Bill and I were in high school at the same time, although I was behind him. He was a handsome fellow and always carried himself well. We were never in the same classes, but I often saw him in the hall. All the students liked Bill. He was a great athlete, and he had such an engaging personality. But, more to the point, I never knew him to take himself seriously."

Before recounting the experiences of Bill's 1947 Golden Bear teammates, to mention Shelbyville Coach Frank Barnes is not only polite, it is imperative. Barnes, or as his friends called him, "Barney," graduated from Roachdale (Indiana) High School in 1921. As a student there, he ran track and played basketball. In 1929, mere months before the onset of The Great Depression, he graduated from Wabash College with both an A. B. and a B. S. Degree. In addition, he earned another degree from Central Normal College.

Barnes coached high school basketball at a series of Indiana schools, namely, Yorktown, Danville, Flora, and Jeffersonville. He coached for one year at Central Normal College in Indianapolis, where his undefeated team won the intercollegiate state title. Over his coaching career, his basketball teams won a string of impressive titles: five sectionals, three regionals, one semi-state, and one state championship. Under his guidance, his teams recorded only two losing seasons over a period of thirty years.

In addition to serving as Shelbyville High School's Head Basketball Coach, he served as its Athletic Director, and as Student Council Sponsor. Morever, he was a very exciting and entertaining Social Studies teacher, who numbered this author among his students. He loved music, woodworking, and teenagers.

All of us who were exposed to his wry sense of humor also knew that behind that charming smile was a man who tolerated absolutely no nonsense in his classroom. As with so many others in this book, each of us is diminished by his death.

When recounting his personal impact on Bill Garrett's life, Coach Barnes' players must speak on his behalf.

Loren "Hank" Hemingway – Teammate, 1947 Shelbyville Golden Bears; Shelbyville High School, 1948; B. S., Education/Accounting, Wichita University (Now Wichita State), 1952; US Military 1952-54; Beech Aircraft, Accounting Division, 1954-55; Whiteland High School Assistant Baseball and Basketball Coach 1955-59; Shelbyville High School Assistant Basketball Coach, 1959-64; Bushnell (Illinois) High School, Head Basketball and Cross Country Coach, 1964-1970; Prudential Insurance 1970-1984; Home Federal Savings Bank, Columbus, Indiana, 1984-1998; retired, Columbus, Indiana:

"I never lost track of Bill after high school graduation. After college, I settled in Shelbyville and taught school. One day, our three-year-old son, Mike, wandered out of the backyard. Frantic, my wife and I searched and searched for the little fellow. We were getting desperate when the telephone rang. It was Bill's mother. I can still hear her voice. 'Hank, I have a little boy over here, and he looks just like you. Have you lost a little boy?'

"Her words were music to my ears. When my wife and I drove over to pick up our son, Laura Garrett brought him out on the porch. She handed him over to me and smiled. I did my best to thank her, but she shushed me and said, 'The minute I saw him, I thought to myself, he looks just like Hank Hemingway. So, I just took him inside and I called you.'

"I don't know what would have happened to our little boy if Mrs. Garrett hadn't spotted him on the sidewalk that afternoon. Nobody would have been surprised at her actions, though. That's the way the Garretts were — open, kind, and loving. Everyone in town respected them. They were a great family."

Bill Breck – Teammate, 1947 Shelbyville Golden Bears; Shelbyville High School, 1947; A. B., DePauw University, 1951; M. S. Education, Indiana University, 1958; Selma High School, 1951-53; Greenfield High School, 1953-58; Principal, Lewisville High School, 1958-60; Principal, Triton Central Schools, Shelby County (7-12), 1960-66; Plainfield High School, 1967-68; Principal, Franklin High School, 1968-84; Hamilton Southeastern Assistant Superintendent, 1984-1994; retired school administrator, Greenwood, Indiana:

"One Christmas vacation, when Bill and I were both home from college, we sat in the Paul Cross Gym locker room — talking about the future. Bill was concerned about his job prospects and commented that there were very few schools that would hire him to coach because of his color. I looked at him and said, 'Bill, don't be overly concerned about that. With your record and reputation, you will do very well.'

"Today, I feel confident that Bill was a strong, positive influence on the students, staff, and parents at Crispus Attucks High School. I regret that Bill cannot join the rest of us 'Bears' when we have our get-togethers. We all miss him. He was a tremendous human being. I know he influenced my life."

Ray Ewick –Teammate Shelbyville Golden Bear Track Team; Shelbyville High School, 1949; US Air Force, Air-Sea Rescue, Denver, Colorado, 1950-52; B. S., Mechanical Engineering, The University of California, Berkeley, 1957; Owens-Illinois Glass Company, Oakland, California, 1952-60; Machine Shop Supervisor, Continental Can, Zanesville, Ohio, 1960-65; Plant Superintendent, Butler Mfg., Visalia, California, 1965-78; Prime Manager, Vasco-Pruden, Turlock, California, 1978-92; retired, Visalia, California:

"Bill was a man whose influence will be long remembered. To this day, I can see his eyes and the expression on his face. He appeared to see the world from a higher plateau and with little better perspective than the rest of us. He was a magnificent athlete and a fine man."

Don Robinson – Teammate, 1947 Shelbyville Golden Bears; Shelbyville High School, 1948; B. S. Mathematics and Physics, Indiana Central College, 1952(Now, The University of Indianapolis); United States Army, White Sands Missile Base Guided Missile Program, 1952-54; taught and coached basketball in a series of small, Southern Indiana high schools 1954-1964; Mathematics and Physics Teacher/Tennis and Track and Field Coach , Arsenal Technical High School, 1965-1990; IUPUI, Department of Mathematics, 1990-1995; retired, Indianapolis, Indiana:

"After high school, we went our separate ways. I went to Indiana Central College, and Bill went to IU. In 1954, I was stationed with the US Army at Fort Bliss, Texas. One day in the barracks, while I read the newspaper, I spotted an article announcing that the Harlem Globetrotters were playing in El Paso the following weekend. I knew that Bill played for the team, so I gathered together a few of my GI friends, and we all went to the game.

"We didn't see Bill play much that evening, because he had broken his wrist in a game the night before. I could understand that. Bill always played hard. We met again later, when I was in summer school at IU. After he introduced me to his wife, Betty, the two of us decided to find an empty court and play a game of tennis.

"Bill liked to play tennis, but it wasn't his best sport. He had just come home from a South American tour with the Globetrotters, and I remember that he said he was getting very tired of all the traveling. He enjoyed the type of game that the team played, but he considered it more 'Show Biz' than '*real*' basketball.

"I saw Bill for the last time at an Eastside Indianapolis YMCA. I was playing tennis there, when I noticed a swim meet getting underway nearby. As I walked over to check it out, I ran into Bill. He was bringing his daughters to the meet. I remember thinking how much dedication it took to accompany children to swim meets. Meets like that took a long time. His presence only reinforced my opinion of him. The young man I grew up with was certainly a dedicated family man."

Walter Wintin – Teammate, 1947 Shelbyville Golden Bears; Shelbyville High School, 1947; Indiana University 1949-50; U. S. Marine Corps, 1948; Indiana University, 1949; U.S. Marine Corps, 1950-52; B. S. Physical Education and Mathematics, Indiana State University, 1955; Master's Degree, Educational Administration, Indiana University, 1960; Head Coach, Football, Wrestling, and Baseball, during the years between 1955 and 1962; Head Wrestling Coach and Mathematics Teacher, Warren Central High School, Indianapolis, 1962-67; Head Wrestling Coach, Seymour High School, 1967-80; Assistant Principal and Athletic Director, Seymour High School, 1980-90; retired, Seymour, Indiana:

"What I remember most about Bill was his temperament. He never showed any outward emotion. He channeled his energies into his game, instead of venting them on his detractors. His 'opening the door' into The Big Ten was no surprise to me at all. He was the perfect person to accomplish that feat. He treated the least talented members of the team as if they were his athletic equals. Nobody I know of ever saw him angry. He was a gentleman when most of us were learning what the word meant. He invited me to his wedding, and

I attended. We were all close — those of us on the team. We are all diminished by his loss."

Clyde Lovellette – Opponent, 1947 High School Championship Game; Terre Haute Garfield, 1948; All-State; 3-time All Conference and All-Wabash Valley; 3-time All-American, The University of Kansas; twice led NCAA in scoring; University of Kansas, 1952; NCAA National Champions, 1952; NCAA Player of the Year, 1952; MVP, NCAA Tournament, 1952; Gold Medalist, United States Olympic Team, 1952; Inductee, The Indiana Basketball Hall of Fame, 1982; White's Institute, Wabash, Indiana; retired, Wabash, Indiana:

"I considered Bill Garrett a class individual in high school. I played against him twice. After I graduated, I visited him at IU, while he played there. I still had the same feeling. I always felt like the two of us could be real 'buddies.' Not many of us, as athletes, ever felt that way about any of our opponents, but I felt that way about Bill. I knew, inside, that I could be really close to him.

"As far as basketball was concerned, Bill was one of the greatest players who ever played in the State of Indiana. Many 'greats' have played in Indiana over the years, both on talented high school teams, and at Indiana University; but, to me, Bill Garrett is up there with the best of them. All you had to do was to be around him for a while and you could see what kind of a character he was. He had a great sense of humor and possessed such incredible talent. It was too bad that he had to pass away at such an early age."

Paul Inlow, M.D. – Shelbyville High School, 1946; Indiana University, 1950; Indiana University School of Medicine, 1956; US Army, Ft. Lee, Virginia, 1960-62; Radiologist and Partner, Inlow Clinic, 1962-1991; Chief Radiologist, W. S. Major Hospital, Shelbyville, Indiana 1991-1996; retired, Shelbyville, Indiana:

"Bill's family was highly respected in Shelbyville. I knew Bill in high school. He was a great guy. Later, we were both at IU at the same time, although I was one year ahead of him. Because neither of us had a car, we arranged to catch rides back and forth to school. My father drove Bill, my wife, Joan, and me back to Bloomington on a number of occasions.

" It was no trouble for us to swing by Bill's house as we headed out of town. While I was an undergraduate in 'pre-med,' my wife and I lived in a trailer. I remember taking Bill home with me after classes one evening. He was a welcome guest in our home, and my wife and I enjoyed his company very much. Throughout his life, he remained the pride of our town."

George Taliaferro – Indiana University, 1951; first Negro NFL Draft Pick; first Negro in NFL history to play quarterback; professional football player, Seattle Seahawks; Special Assistant to President John Ryan, Indiana University, 1972-82; Indiana University faculty until retirement; retired, Bloomington, Indiana:

"I enrolled at Indiana University in the summer of 1945, and during the 1945-46 season, I played on the only Indiana University football team to ever compile an undefeated season and win the Big Ten Football Championship. Uncle Sam drafted me in 1946, and discharged me in June of 1947. When

I returned to campus, I met a freshman basketball recruit named Bill Garrett. At that time, the total complement of Negro students numbered about one hundred. Because of the limited social activities, the entire Negro student body was a well-oiled social machine in and of itself.

"When Bill entered the IU basketball program, he found less than a total level of acceptance on the part of the other players. Phil Buck and Gene Ring formed the first two of an iron triangle later completed by Bill Tosheff. Those friends insulated Bill from a lot of trouble, and they would have defended him in a millisecond.

"Ring graduated from South Bend Central High School in 1947, where he was captain of three sports as a senior — football, baseball, and basketball. An All-State basketball player, he played under two Hall of Fame Coaches. Their names were John Wooden and Bob Primmer.

"Coach McCracken recognized the real 'find' he had in Bill. Campus acceptance blossomed as the student body witnessed Bill's incredible talent on the court. At the height of Bill's career at IU, the students treated him as if he were any other player. There was never a hint of difference because of his race. Had he been any other ethnicity but Negro, it would have made no difference at all. The IU students adored him.

"On the more private side, I knew Bill very well. His opportunity to play basketball for Indiana University thrilled him, and he meant to perform as well as he could, irrespective of any venue in which he found himself. Branch explained the significance of his position on the team — not only was he the first Negro to play basketball at IU, but he was also the first Negro to play basketball in The Big Ten Conference. Pressure never bothered Bill, but the importance of his role wasn't lost on him, either.

"We had a lot in common, in terms of our careers. We

both played a varsity sport at Indiana, we both served in the military, and we both went on to play professional sports after we earned our degrees. I only wish that more young people had had the pleasure of knowing Bill. He was one of the most incredible athletes that the world ever knew. A magnificent basketball player, he also excelled in track and field.

"As far as 'firsts' were concerned, Bill and I had something else in common.

"In 1949, I was not only the first Negro to be drafted by the National Football League, but I was also the first Negro in NFL history to play the quarterback position.

"Bill and I lost track of each other after college. He played for the Harlem Globetrotters, and I played for one team that changed its name five times in six years. Ultimately, at the end of my 'pro' career, I played for the Seattle Seahawks.

"In 1972, I returned to Bloomington and served as Special Assistant to the Indiana University President. One day in 1974 — I think it was in either March or April — Bill called me at my office. He wondered if we could pull together a reunion for all the Black Indiana University alumni. He was very serious about it, and I could tell that he had given the topic a lot of thought.

"Looking back on that conversation, I feel Bill must have had some sort of a premonition about his own death. Mortality took a heavy toll on Indiana's Black educators that year. Not long after we lost Bill, we also lost Jim Ballow, an excellent school administrator in Indianapolis.

"After Bill died, I thought about his quest for a peer reunion, and I decided to do something about it. One day, I looked at my secretary and vowed that I wouldn't let Bill Garrett's dream die with him. After a great deal of work, I witnessed his dream come to life. In 1977, nearly three years after Bill's death, Indiana University hosted a reunion in

Bloomington for all its African-American alumni — both undergraduate and graduate.

"Those of us involved in the organization and promotion of the event researched every single publication having any connection with the university in order to avoid omitting even one person. In that vein, we followed the wise words of another astute Indiana University personality. In the words of Chancellor Herman B Wells, 'So long as a student attends Indiana University even one day, that person is considered an alumnus.'

"When I went to the Indiana High School Basketball Finals in 1947, I saw Bill and the Shelbyville Golden Bears defeat Clyde Lovellette and his tremendous Terre Haute Garfield team. I knew that Indiana needed to recruit the Shelbyville center. The committee functioned. Indiana agreed. Bill came.

"With regard to Bill Garrett's personality, he was almost beyond passive. He talked very little, but he listened carefully. Make no mistake about it — in spite of his outward manner, Bill was a most observant person. He took in everything. He was an exacting person. He didn't embellish his speech with unnecessary words. When he said something, there was no need for his audience to interpret what he said. To me, he was plain spoken, but perfectly clear — in a word, precise.

"Bill had the face of an angel and the demeanor of a choir boy. His voice was soft and kind in tone. Yet, underneath that outward portrait, beat the heart of a fierce competitor. When opponents tried to defeat him by harshly attacking him on the court, they received a tough response paired with a calm facial expression.

"His body language never hinted at his ability to gain the advantage over an opponent. Instead, Bill's classic response to such aggression was a level of performance seldom seen in collegiate sports. When other players challenged him, he defeated them. If I had been a basketball player, I would have wanted to be on 'his good side.' In one sentence, Bill let his game do his talking.

"I grieve that today's youth have no role model as sterling as Bill Garrett. His mentoring ability left a benchmark few can equal, let alone surpass. His ability to connect with the young people in his care speaks volumes in terms of heart, let alone character. I consider Bill Garrett one of the finest men I ever had the privilege to know."

James Roberson, M.D.* – Bill Garrett's Indiana University roommate; Indiana University, 1950; Indiana University School of Medicine, 1953; Gynecologist-Obstetrician; retired, Rochester, New York:

"Bill was extremely shy when we first met. I 'hit the books' every night, because I wanted to get into medical school on a scholarship. I majored in anatomy and physiology, so my class load was both heavy and difficult. I felt that my habits rubbed off on Bill, because, in a few weeks, he began to study the minute he returned to our room after supper. We were both close to our families, and we both wanted to succeed.

"I know now that, during college, we both accepted things that we never should have accepted. As a consequence, we suffered the degradation and humiliation heaped upon us in silence.

"We stayed in touch over the years. He had a tremendous career in coaching and teaching. We both worked at progressively higher levels of our professions. He began as a high school coach, moved up to athletic director, and ended his career as a college administrator. In like fashion, after several years of general practice and a residency at St. Mary's Hospital in Rochester, New York, I completed a fellowship in Obstetrics and Gynecology at King's County Hospital in New York City. Upon completion of that training, I opened an OB-GYN practice in Rochester.

"Racially speaking, our careers also paralleled one another. At the pinnacle of his career, Bill was an Assistant Dean on a predominately white campus, and I was an obstetrician-gynecologist with a practice serving predominately white patients. In solid numbers, my practice was 65% white. Our successes were based on similar values — a deep sense of commitment to hard work and a sincere desire to achieve a goal.

"When Bill died, I traveled to Indiana for his funeral. I did my best to explain to Betty and the children exactly how and why he died. That is the hardest part of medicine — knowing that there is nothing that you, or others like you, can do — given the circumstances. I mourn his loss. He set a high mark for his players, his students, and his advisees. We are greatly diminished by his passing. As a role model, I can think of no one better. He was a good friend and a very fine man."

*Dr. James Roberson died January 6, 2001, in Rochester, New York. On December 27, 2000, he and his beloved wife, Alice, celebrated their 48th Wedding Anniversary. He graciously granted interviews throughout the preparation of this book. His insights into Bill's psyche and his near "total recall" of timely facts added a great deal of substance to this work.

The author considers his contributions priceless.

Hetty Gray

Hallie Bryant and Bill Garrett shared many things in common, not the least of which was the title of Indiana's "Mr. Basketball," awarded to Bill in 1947 and to Hallie in 1953. In addition, Ray Crowe linked the two men. Hallie graduated from Crispus Attucks High School, where he played for Coach Ray Crowe, and Bill eventually took Crowe's place as Head Coach of the Tigers.

Not only did both men play for the IU Hurryin' Hoosiers, but they also went on to play for The Harlem Globetrotters. Hallie's career with the Globetrotters lasted an impressive twenty-seven years — thirteen as a player and fourteen in the front office with the Public Relations Department.

His consistently successful and well-received motivational presentation, dubbed "A One-man Harlem Globetrotter Show," provided the foundation for his contemporary motivational programs tailored to business and industry. Their focus? How to achieve and maintain harmony in the workplace.

Hallie Bryant – close personal friend of Bill Garrett; Indiana High School Basketball Tournament Final Four, 1951; Indiana's "Mr. Basketball," 1953; Indiana All-Star, 1953; named Star of Stars, 1953; Crispus Attucks High School, 1953; Indiana University, 1957; In seventeen years with the Harlem Globetrotters, he circled the globe three times and appeared in 82 nations; Inductee, Indiana Basketball Hall of Fame, 1983; currently a motivational speaker, Indianapolis, Indiana:[34]

"I met Bill Garrett for the first time when I was in the seventh grade. At that time, 'Sonny' Boyd worked with the organizers of 'The Dust Bowl Tournament,' a basketball competition held at Lockefield Gardens in Indianapolis. I played against Bill Garrett, Marshall Murray, and Emerson Johnson during that series. All three of them were older than I was at the time, but I gave it my best shot. In the end, they beat us by only three points.

"Bill was a masterpiece in terms of his professionalism. He had big shoes to fill when he took over Coach Crowe's position at Attucks, yet he handled that challenge like he did all the others in his life — he handled it with class. On a personal level, I really knew Bill's wife first. I became acquainted with Betty when she coached at an Indianapolis YWCA. She did a wonderful job there, and she earned a high reputation in her own right. They were a good team.

"It's hard to calculate Bill's contribution when it comes to the Black players who followed him in collegiate basketball. To me, Bill was a real 'pathfinder.' I never heard him say an ill word about anyone, although, in many circumstances, he had very good reason to do so. He put himself 'on the line' for all of us. As an educator, I'd describe Bill in terms of what I call 'The Four L's, — Learning, Living, Loving, and Legacy.' He excelled in each."

Albert Spurlock – close personal friend of Bill Garrett; B. S., Education, The University of Illinois, 1938; M. S., Education, The University of Illinois, 1939; Industrial Arts Teacher and Track Coach, Crispus Attucks High School; retired, Indianapolis, Indiana:

"I headed the Industrial Arts Department at Crispus Attucks High School. In addition to teaching 'shop,' I served as Head Coach of the Attucks Tigers Track Team. Bill Garrett acted as my Assistant Coach during the track season. Bill's accomplishments as a high school and college track star made him a valuable addition to my coaching staff. However, our time at Attucks was not the genesis of our association.

"My knowledge of Bill Garrett dated back to 1947, when Bill DeFrantz, Director of the Fall Creek YMCA, called upon me, and a number of others, to help him in an effort to encourage Indiana University to recruit the current Indiana 'Mr. Basketball' for its athletic program. 'Mr. Basketball, 1947' was, of course, Bill Garrett, star center of the 1947 State Champion Shelbyville Golden Bears.

"The group consisted of DeFrantz, Hopson Ziegler, Rufus Kuykendall, Everett Hall, and me. We traveled to Bloomington and met with President Herman B Wells in his office. During that meeting, we all did our best to explain to President Wells that Conference schools allowed Negro players to participate on freshman teams, but cut them from varsity rosters when varsity positions were awarded. He listened very attentively to our comments, and he promised us he would 'look into the matter right away.' We left with good feelings, but we didn't make Indiana University our last stop.

"The next Saturday, we traveled to West Lafayette and talked with Purdue University officials about the same subject. As a result of our efforts, and those of white IU alumni from Shelbyville, Bill entered Indiana University the next fall. I might add, though, that in 1948, Purdue University, too, recruited a talented Negro player from Kokomo. Finally, the Big Ten Conference was open to Negro athletes in more than football and track. Basketball, the sole holdout, had finally opened up to them as well.

"As far as Bill's work at Attucks was concerned, I feel that he shared a great many personal characteristics with Ray Crowe, his predecessor. Both men were quiet and worked beautifully with their players. In Bill's case, I would say that his players literally worshipped him. What's more, all the students had a great deal of respect for Bill. Take, for example, this typical, school day behavioral situation.

"If Bill walked down the hall and spotted a student out of class, he didn't have to say a word. All he had to do was point his finger. One look at Coach Garrett's facial expression and his outstretched finger was all it took to compel the errant student — boy or girl — to return to wherever he or she was supposed to be at the time. Bill was a powerful influence in the high school building, whether he was in the hall, in the classroom, or in the gymnasium.

"During lunch, all our Attucks teachers ate at a table in one particular area of the school cafeteria. I noted that when Bill talked, he omitted one particular phase of his basketball career. He talked about high school and college athletics, but he seldom mentioned his stint with the Harlem Globetrotters. I remember that questioners had to literally pry information out of him about his travels with that team.

"On a more personal note, Bill was fiercely loyal to his friends and to his players. He would 'go to bat' for anyone if he thought the situation merited his intervention. He took it upon himself to size up a problem and take it on. As an advocate, he had a lot of clout from a professional standpoint, yet he never was one to 'throw his weight around.' In the end, his ability and professionalism spoke for themselves. I felt privileged to work with him. He was a fine man."

Theodore Boyd – West Virginia State College, 1947; Senate Avenue YMCA Executive; 'Dust Bowl Tournament' organizer; Hoosier author and poet; retired, Indianapolis, Indiana:

"I worked at the Senate Avenue 'Y' when a group of us

organized an invitational basketball tournament for youngsters at Lockefield Gardens, near downtown Indianapolis. A
team drove up from Shelbyville. Among the players were
three of the boys who played on the 1947 State Champion
Golden Bears. Those boys were tough competitors, but they
were fair competitors. In the end, they beat us by only three
points. I met Bill Garrett that day, and I liked him immediately.

"Later, he came to visit me at Attucks. We shared many
nice conversations, and we spoke about a lot of different subjects — not strictly basketball. I always took an interest in
young people, and that's one thing I can say about Crispus
Attucks High School. We had one of the best staffs around.

"We had a lifetime friendship, Bill and I. He is no longer
with us, but his melody lingers on. To me, Bill was the epitome
of a man who possessed the talents of an 'all around teacher.'
He excelled in every single phase of his life. He was so
competent...so caring...so unassuming...so admired.... He
carried himself well and evidenced absolutely no hint of ego.

"Bill stressed a solid philosophy. He encouraged those
with whom he worked to be the very best they could be —
mentally, physically, and spiritually. In turn, he passed those
values on through his coaching. Every player who worked
under him was better off for the experience."

Don Thomas – B. S. Education, Indiana Central College,
1956; M. A., Educational Administration, Butler University,
1960; Assistant Basketball Coach at Crispus Attucks under
Bill Garrett and his replacement as Head Coach of the Tigers
when Bill resigned to take the position of Athletic Director;
close personal friend; retired, Indianapolis, Indiana:

Net Prophet: The Bill Garrett Story

"Bill Garrett, to my mind, was an ideal person. He enjoyed teaching business and coaching basketball. Teaching offered him the opportunity to work with girls. He taught typing in the business department, and few boys enrolled in that class. I'm sure that his competitive spirit spilled over into his typing contests and drills among his students. I remember that when class schedules were assigned to teachers, he always hoped that he retained his typing class.

"Bill's character and morals were of the highest caliber. His firmly held values and priorities carried over to the boys he coached. He was generous and understanding. His players knew that if they brought their personal problems to him, he would listen and try to help them resolve the situations in a positive way. A considerate man, he imparted good instincts to his players. His influence motivated many of his students to achieve at high levels later in life."

(As Bill's assistant, Don had a "bench view" of Bill Garrett, the coach. Don's comments are especially cogent, because they come from someone who worked hand in hand with Bill when he was Head Coach at Crispus Attucks.)

"Bill gave me a lot of leeway in my job. He accepted my ideas politely and considered them thoughtfully. When he implemented some of my ideas, he always complemented me on my contributions. I recall him saying — more than once, too —'That's a good idea. I hadn't thought of that.'

"In many ways, Bill was a father figure to his players and to many of those younger teachers with whom he worked. He considered sports a wonderful outlet for young people, an outlet in which he, personally, could wield some personal guidance in an attractive venue. To those of us who watched him in action, he accomplished a great deal. His personality not only made an impression on his players, but it rubbed off on them in a very personal way."

Ray Crowe – Whiteland High School, 1930 — twice leading scorer and captain of the Whiteland team; Four-letterman at Indiana Central College; Indiana Central College, 1938 (Now the University of Indianapolis); Head Coach and Athletic Director, Crispus Attucks High School, Indianapolis, Indiana, 1950-57; Crispus Attucks Athletic Director, 1957-71; Inductee, Indiana Basketball Hall of Fame, 1968; retired, Indianapolis:[35]

"I coached seventh and eighth grade basketball at School No. 17 before I took the job as Head Basketball Coach at Crispus Attucks in 1950. I continued to coach the Tigers until the end of the 1956-57 season, when I decided to make a job change. The administrators at Attucks began to search for my replacement. Many applications came into the athletic office. When the process ended, school authorities selected Bill Garrett. At that time, Bill was Head Basketball Coach for Harry E. Wood High School. He replaced me in the fall of 1957.

"After retiring from coaching, I assumed the position of Attucks Athletic Director. In that job, I worked very closely with Bill. I was extremely fond of him. We shared a good working relationship. The entire student body respected Bill, on and off the basketball court.

"He did an excellent job as Head Coach at Attucks High School, and he led our Tigers to the State Championship in 1959. His background in basketball more than prepared him for a successful career in coaching. In sum, I believe that he did a very good job at Crispus Attucks High School."

Edgar Searcy – played for Ray Crowe on the 1956 State Champion Crispus Attucks Tigers; played one year for Bill Garrett; Crispus Attucks High School, 1958; Indiana All-Star, 1958; Indiana Star of Stars, 1958; Two-letterman at The University of Illinois; B. S., Accounting, Southern Illinois University, 1966; J. D., Indiana University School of Law, Indianapolis, 1990; retired Eli Lilly & Company CPA; practicing attorney, Indianapolis, Indiana:[36]

"I played for Bill Garrett during his first year as Head Coach at Crispus Attucks High School. In many ways, he was much more a friend to me than a coach. He was an excellent basketball coach, to be sure, but, to my mind, he came across as someone who was far more than a teacher.

"After I graduated from high school, my relationship with him grew even closer. My first college experience was at The University of Illinois, where I played forward on the basketball team. However, I returned home to work for two and a half years before returning to school. I enrolled at Southern Illinois University, where I also played basketball. I usually played forward, but, occasionally, I played center.

"I kept in close touch with Coach Garrett during college. He was extremely easy to talk to, and I knew that if I encountered a problem in college, I could go to him for advice. He was a very understanding person. When he listened to me, he gave me his undivided attention.

"Although we did not see each other socially, we maintained a solid, strong friendship as adults. Speaking from a player's point of view, he was a good role model."

Hetty Gray

Harry Larrabee — Shelbyville High School Class of 1970; Indiana High School All-Star Team, 1970; The University of Texas, 1975; Captain, the University of Texas Basketball team; All-Conference Honors and two-time participant in the NCAA Championship Tournament; Head Coach, Southwest Texas State for five years; Head Coach and Administrator, The University of Alaska, 17 years; an original organizer of "The Great Alaska Shootout" Tournament; Head Basketball Coach, Shelbyville Golden Bears:

Larrabee recounts a one-on-one conversation with Bill Garrett in 1970:

"I played guard for the Shelbyville Golden Bears under Coach Carl Hughes during high school. In our final game of the 1970 season, we played a hard-fought, physical game against the Crispus Attucks Tigers at Attucks High School. We lost a very close contest (92-85).

"It was a bruising loss for all of us, and disappointment hung in the air as we sat in the locker room after the game. Unexpectedly, Crispus Attucks Athletic Director Bill Garrett,walked in the locker room door.

"After he spoke with Head Coach Carl Hughes and some of the other players, he walked to my side and put his arm around me. I remember that game well. The atmosphere in the gym was very tense. Racial moods were heightened at the time, and the home crowd was 'on edge,' to put it mildly.

"With his arm still around my shoulder, he guided me to a corner of the room. Not only was I crestfallen after the loss, but I was shocked at what was happening to me at that particular moment. I was mesmerized by the fact that this man, who had been the pride of my hometown since the 1940s, Indiana's 'Mr. Basketball,' a legendary trailblazer for Blacks in America, and a basketball star at Indiana University — *this* man was taking me aside for a personal conversation.

"I said little, but I listened intently. I remember his voice. It was soft in tone. There was no hint of ego in his manner. I tried to come to grips with the fact that I was in the presence of a man I had idolized for years. I stood in awe of his accomplishments, and the next few minutes only increased my respect for him.

"He talked with me with the sincerity of a friend, the wisdom of a father, and the empathy of an athlete who had known the pain of losing an extremely physical game. He not only complimented me on my performance in the game*, but he also lauded my sportsmanship. *(Larrabee scored 36 points before fouling out.)

"He wished me the very best for my collegiate career, emphasizing that he, too, had strong ties to Shelbyville High School. His manner of speaking was soothing.... encouraging...uplifting...inspirational....

"My memories of that night remain as vivid today as they were later that same night, on the drive home. I drew tremendously on that experience when I played in college. More importantly, I drew on it every time I coached. In essence, he taught me more about life that night than about basketball. Such actions by an opposing athletic director in the visitors' locker room were rare indeed.

"That summer I played on the Indiana All-Star Team. Our Assistant Coach was Hallie Bryant. The link between us was Bill Garrett — and what a link he was.

"Today, I realize the significance of that night. His words reinforced the importance of honor, integrity, and sportsmanship, yet his actions went even further. As busy as he was, he took the time to take a young player aside and have a genuine, sincere conversation with him. He spoke from the heart, and his eyes conveyed a kindness I will never forget. Weighty as his words, however, was his demeanor.

"Every nuance of Bill Garrett's mannerisms exuded humility. I can think of no higher character trait more worthy of aspiration. The effects of our chance meeting not only continue to inspire me, but they hone my coaching techniques to this day."

Steve Downing – played under Hall of Fame Coach Bill Green on the undefeated 1969 Indiana State Champion Washington Continentals; Indianapolis Washington High School, 1969; Indiana High School All Stars, 1969; Indiana University, 1973; first All-Big Ten Basketball Player under IU Coach Bob Knight; First Big Ten "MVP" since Archie Dees in 1958; First Round Draft Choice for The Boston Celtics; Forward for The Boston Celtics, 1973-75; Member, 1994 Silver Anniversary Team; Chosen as Indiana University's first Black athletic administrator, 1980; Associate Athletic Director, Indiana University, Bloomington, Indiana:[37]

"I consider Bill Garrett a true pioneer. He not only paved the way for me, but for every other Black Indiana University basketball player who came before or after me. I followed him, but, more precisely, he led me. Whenever I walked out onto the court at IU, I thought of all the things he had done to make it possible for me to do so.

"He has always been an inspiration to me. I don't think that there has been a day in my professional life when I haven't thought about Bill. There is no doubt in my mind that his trailblazing lay the foundation for Black athletic administrators, as well as players. He was, and is, the ultimate role model for young Black men."

Mike Davis – University of Alabama, 1983; Milwaukee Bucks' Second Round Draft Pick; played basketball in Switzerland and Italy, 1983-85 and named to the European League's All-Star team; Topeka Sizzlers, Continental Basketball Association, 1988-89; Assistant Coach, Miles College, Birmingham, Alabama, 1989-90; Coached for Venezuelan National Basketball Team for two summers; coached Venezuelan professional basketball teams; worked under current Indiana Associate Head Coach John Treloar with the CBA's Wichita Falls Texans, 1990-94; Chicago Rockers, 1994-95; Assistant Coach under Bob Knight, Indiana University, 1997; Head Basketball Coach, Indiana University, Bloomington, Indiana:[38]

Although more than thirty years separated their careers, Bill Garrett and Mike Davis share unique athletic credentials. They were both named "Mr. Basketball" for their respective states, Bill for Indiana in 1947 and Mike for Alabama in 1983. Each man earned collegiate All-American status while in college. In addition, not only did each of them post a new scoring record for his particular Alma Mater, but each man also graduated from college with a B. S. in Physical Education.

The two were selected by major NBA teams in the early rounds of the professional draft, but, as a result of different circumstances, each of them played basketball overseas — Bill for the US Army in Korea and Mike for a professional basketball league in Europe. Culminating exemplary careers in the professional ranks of the sport, the two men returned to either high school or college levels to coach young men in the sport they loved.

Hetty Gray

In Mike Davis' words...

"Bill Garrett is a legendary Indiana University basketball player. I have had the pleasure to meet his wife and his son. They are good people. Billy is a Christian fellow, open and kind. He has quite a heritage, and he is currently an assistant basketball coach at Seton Hall.

"Bill Garrett endured a great deal when he played for Indiana in the late 1940s and early 1950s. It took a lot of courage for him to step forward and put himself in that position. So many men remain in his debt. He virtually paved the way for every Black basketball player at Indiana University — all those who have played here since his pioneering season and all those who will play here in the future."

Chapter Sixteen

B etty and the children paint an intimate and touching portrait of Bill Garrett, the family man. Their memories portray a very intensely personal side of a public man. In a day when Black fatherhood is assailed from every quarter, when the Black family is labeled at high risk, and when so many Black children grow up without a father in the home, Bill Garrett's life shines like a candle in the darkness. His is a life that achieved that rare and delicate balance between career and family.

Listed first — in order of age, eldest to youngest — are the children's descriptions of their father. In a series of candid cameos, their stories are tinged with the simple details of their youth, yet each of their contributions emphasizes the bond they shared with a devoted father. Then, in closing, Betty condenses her precious memories into a single paragraph — a fitting tribute to a man of few words and big deeds.

Tina Louise Garrett - Shortridge High School, 1974 ; B. S., Industrial Management, Indiana University, 1979; J. D., John Marshall Law School, Chicago, Illinois, 1984; Chicago area attorney, specializing in litigation and family law:

"Our family revolved around faith and fun. While my mother was the more vocal of our parents, my father was the quiet strength — the core of our family. Those who considered a coach as a very "macho" person would have been very surprised to see my father in the kitchen. He got up early every school day and cooked breakfast for all us children. I remember that he cooked a lot of different dishes for us. Among them were bacon and eggs, pancakes, hot Cream of Wheat, and really good oatmeal.

"Dad was handy around the house. Because of his example, I enjoy keeping my own house in good repair today. He could fix anything, and he made a real effort to keep everything running smoothly. He was really busy during the school year, as we were. So, when school let out, he made sure that our summers were filled with fun.

"The focal point of every summer was our vacation. My father planned all our vacations. Before our younger brother was born, we three girls had the entire back seat to ourselves. We liked to rest while he drove, but the seat didn't give us all enough room to lie down. Consequently, Dad leveled out the floorboard of our family Oldsmobile. To flatten out the hump in the carpet, he made a plywood platform so one of us could sleep down there. Before we left home, we called out our choice, 'seat' or 'floor.'

"One of my favorite trips was to Pennsylvania, Virginia, Maryland, and Washington, D. C. My parents wanted us to know more about American history, so they took us to see the Liberty Bell, Betsy Ross' home, Mount Vernon, Baltimore, The Smithsonian Institution, and all the famous monuments in the Washington area. I can't remember all the places we went that summer, but it was the most wonderful trip of my life, and my Dad made sure that we girls understood the significance of all the places we visited along the way.

"Most of our trips were uneventful, but one was a bit harrowing, now that I look back on it. I was in the restroom of a filling station when my mother came in and told me to get to the car 'right now.' I didn't know what was wrong, but I knew she meant business, so I hurried and climbed into the back seat with my sisters.

"A group of 'rednecks' were harassing my father. Ever the family defender, Dad recognized a hostile situation and sought to get away quickly. I remember my Dad rolling down the driver's window and saying something to the men.

"All of a sudden, the men were in a vehicle next to ours, but aimed in the opposite direction. Dad pulled away and drove down the road. The men wheeled their car around and chased us, but Dad managed to elude them. I've never forgotten it. I knew that Dad had protected us that day, but I didn't understand the perilous degree of the incident. It was a very dangerous predicament, but he handled it so well that we were never scared. He showed no fear at all. He was our champion.

"We knew that Dad was involved in sports, but that wasn't his identity to us. He was just our Dad. Today, I know he used his coaching skills with us all the time. He played a big part in our own athletics, when we were growing up. We swam a lot in competition, and our parents always accompanied us to the weekend events.

"At first, when Dad went to a swim meet, he just sat and watched — but that didn't last very long. Dad was never one to sit on the sidelines, so he took classes in his spare time and became an official starter. In time, he fired the gun at most of our meets.

"He taught all of us girls to drive. I remember that he took me out to a big parking lot on Saturday and he gave me instructions, step by step. He was a good teacher. I didn't take the Drivers' Education course before I got my license. My father had already taught me all the skills I needed to know.

"Dad played Santa Claus at Christmas time. He had a big, red suit — wig and all. He'd dress up and sneak downstairs to surprise us. Our little brother, Billy, squealed with delight when he saw Santa suddenly appear. I remember seeing Dad in the backyard with Billy. I think Billy must have been about four years old. Dad was teaching him to play basketball. It was just precious to watch them together.

"We always had dinner together, even with Dad's hectic schedule. On practice nights, he'd come home late. We'd have a snack to hold us over until he came home, and it wasn't unusual for us to eat around eight o'clock. I can remember being at the table at nearly nine o'clock. We always talked together at the dinner table. Both our parents placed a high value on eating together as a family.

"One of the most important gifts I received from my parents was a good sense of who I was. They were comfortable with who and what they were, and they passed that confidence along to me. Seeing that characteristic in my parents inspired it in me.

"Dad was a risk taker, and he never let us think that life could defeat us. He always encouraged us to 'keep going.' He was committed to our family, and he encouraged all of us children to earn our spending money by working around the house.

"He used to pay us a penny for every dandelion we could dig up in the yard. I would work and work to see if I could dig up fifty of them. Fifty cents bought candy when I was a little girl, and I felt good to have my own money to spend.

"In addition to being an AAU Director, he also worked in the public arena. The Governor of Indiana appointed him to a position with The Department of Natural Resources. He traveled around and inspected various state facilities on the weekends. I remember that he took me to several different state parks with him, and he even taught me to fish.

"With regard to education, my father was a very involved parent, but so was my mother. Both my parents took very supportive roles with us girls at home, but for most of our school days, neither my mother nor my father found it necessary to defend us publicly. An essay contest changed all that for me.

"When I was in high school, a large Indianapolis corporation sponsored an essay contest with a large cash prize. With my teacher's encouragement, I entered the competition. I had an advisor at school, but she didn't help me a lot. As a result, I did a great deal of work on my own. I researched and wrote a very lengthy paper on 'The Buffalo Soldiers' of the nineteenth century American West.

"When I turned the paper in, the judges claimed that I had not written the paper without help. They accused me of plagiarism. Only two students in the entire high school submitted entries in the contest, and the judges disqualified my work on ethical grounds. Their decision spurred my father to action.

"At that time, he was Assistant Dean out at IUPUI. He took my paper to a professor there and asked him to review it. The professor found small errors in organization and formatting, but he confirmed that all my facts were correct. In his words, he considered the meat of the paper to be 'factual,' not 'plagiarist.'

"Next, My father called Shortridge and arranged a meeting with the appropriate school officials. When he arrived, he had the professor's critique 'in hand.' After much discussion, he learned that the other student's paper lacked real quality. Despite his protestations, my paper remained disqualified, as did the paper of the other student. There was no winner at Shortridge, in terms of the contest.

"Yet, I felt, in a greater sense, that I won. Why? Because my father believed me…because my father trusted me…because my father was willing to fight for me…because my father knew that I was right and the school officials were wrong….

"As an attorney who litigates family law in courtrooms on a regular basis, I understand the pressures put on today's young people. Every day, I internalize my concept of 'family' from personal experience. For that reason, my childhood has a direct bearing on my work. My family's values not only strengthen me as a person, but they also frustrate me as an attorney working regularly with people in dire straits.

"I encounter crises on a daily basis. Most frequently, these circumstances involve either divorce or criminal activity. My clients' stress levels are excruciating, and their pain affects me profoundly. I draw from a deep well in terms of supporting my clients. I learned how to listen at the feet of my father, and I try to follow in his footsteps.

"My father was an excellent listener. I know his spirit and his teachings guide me as I work with people in trouble. Often, when I feel I cannot spare the time, I *take* the time to really listen to my clients. Sometimes, that's all they really need. I often work on behalf of the guilty, in contrast to only defending the innocent. In mere seconds, a hasty act borne out of foolishness or inattention can wreck an entire life

"In the course of counseling a client, I attempt to explain the after effects of his or her actions. That is, I try to strike a balance between how the crime affected my client and how it affected the victim and the victim's family. I emphasize to my client how he or she can move on in the aftermath of an ugly scrape with the law.

"To that end, I utilize many of the tactics I observed my

father employ as I watched him when I was a child. When he talked with people, he gave them his undivided attention. He listened to them, and he asked lots of probing questions in order to have a better grasp of their circumstances. I firmly believe that his listening style induced people to pay close attention to his response.

"My brother's coaching career sparks achievement from his players. Here in Chicago, I remain in close contact with a young man who played basketball for my brother at Chicago's Providence-St. Mel High School. Today, he is twenty-two years old, he works full-time, and he has his own apartment. One of six children, he is the first and only one of his siblings to graduate from high school. I am convinced that this young man will have a quality life because my brother took the time to work with him.

"Such is our legacy. All of us learned at the knee of a master. Our father taught us that compassion and concern are meaningless unless they are put to good use. What's more, he taught us that only love has the power to change lives."

Judith Ann Garrett Shelton – Shortridge High School, 1975; Purdue University, 1976; Texas Southern University, School of Pharmacy, Houston, Texas, 1982; Doctorate in Pharmacy, 1998; Pharmacist, Houston, Texas; married, mother of five children (three girls and two boys, ages three to seventeen):

"Dad loved to play with us. We'd go over to Butler University and sled down the steep hill. We had a big wooden sled with red letters on it. When we were very small, he'd ride on the sled with us. After we were bigger, he'd put us all on the sled and watch us slide down the hill. In so many ways, my father bathed us all with an unconditional love that I will never forget.

"He taught me to ride a bike. He put me on the pink bike and said, 'Hold on, Judy!' He held me steady on the sidewalk. He ran behind me — pushing the bike — encouraging me, saying, 'Pedal, Judy! Pedal the bike!' I can hear his voice just as if it were yesterday. Tears come to my eyes whenever I think of it.

"Dad took the whole family on bike rides around the neighborhood. My sisters and I always rode faster than our parents did — especially when we rode through the bike trails on the Butler University campus. We also rode pretty fast on the side streets. It was family fun, and, as a kid, I loved it.

"Dad let us sleep in the car on Saturday mornings on the way to our swim meets. When it was my turn to swim, Dad would lean down and say, 'Judy, just do your best!' I knew he would be watching me, and I always did my best.

"Dad was a quiet man, but one always felt his presence in a room. I remember how strongly that I felt his presence the day of his funeral. That day, someone told us that cars were still turning out of the church parking lot when the hearse carrying my father, and the car directly behind it carrying our family, made the last turn toward the main gates of Crown Hill Cemetery.

"I don't know exactly how many cars were behind us that day, but the number had to be high. After all, it was almost a mile and a half from the front of The Witherspoon Presbyterian Church to the corner on West 38th Street, where the funeral procession turned east toward the cemetery's main entrance.

"I can tell you that day was the saddest day of my life — the day they buried my father. What I didn't know then was that the whole stigma of losing a parent to heart disease would thrust me into the medical field.

"I never knew, and I don't even know to this day if my mother knew it, but Dad was under a doctor's care. Looking back, I wonder if he took his medicine on a regular basis. I also question if he understood the importance of taking his regular medication, even when he felt well.

"Those haunting questions have made me a better professional. I have worked as a pharmacist for several years now, and, whenever I run into one of my former patients around Houston, they are happy to see me. Perhaps, that is because I take a great deal of time in explaining to them exactly what their medication is and precisely how to take it in order to gain the greatest benefit from its ingredients.

"There's a hint of my Dad in the future right here in Houston today — our three-year-old son, Garrett. He actually has a nickname. We call him 'Mister Bill.' Not only does he look exactly like my Dad, but he can also handle a basketball! My Dad's promise still lives. He would have been so proud of his grandchildren, and he really would have been surprised at my composure when I wrestle with our five, distinctly different children.

"Knowing myself as I do," she said, with a chuckle, "I am convinced that my levels of patience have to come from somewhere else. I never thought I'd have the patience that I have today. Quite frankly, I credit it to my upbringing. When I talked to my Dad, I saw unconditional love in his eyes. What's more, I knew that when I talked with him, I had his undivided attention. I try to impart that to my children as well as to my patients."

Laurie Jean Garrett — Shortridge High School, 1977; B. S., Mathematics, Syracuse University, 1984; Master's Degree in Divinity, Princeton Theological Seminary, 1988; Master's of Theology, Princeton Theological Seminary, 1989; Credentialed as a Clinical Pastoral Education Supervisor, C.P.E., 2000; Pastoral Counseling Supervisor, The Carolina Medical Center, Charlotte, North Carolina:

"It has been a long time since my father died, and yet I still find it difficult to talk about him. He was a great father to us children and a wonderful husband to our mother. I never knew him as an athlete. That identity never had any meaning for me. To me, he was simply my father.

"He did everything well. I adored him, and yet, as an adult, I view my feelings as far more than a daughter's simple idolatry for her father. My feelings go much deeper than that. My father loved to laugh. He played with us girls a lot when we were children. He was always available to us, and he was an incredibly thoughtful man, and he never forgot our birthdays.

"I especially remember my 14th birthday — actually, it was the year before he died. He took me shopping. We went out — just the two of us. He took me to a jewelry store and bought me a necklace. It was beautiful. Four letters hung on it. They spelled 'love.' There was a little diamond in the center of the 'o.' He made me feel so incredibly special.

"His laughter? How do I remember his laughter? Well, it started in his eyes. His eyes would sparkle, then a big grin would spread out over his face. He would chuckle, and then that chuckle would burst into raucous, wonderful laughter. He was a quiet, humble man, but he knew how to smile and laugh with us. In my heart, I know that he enjoyed his family tremendously.

"We all used to sit down, as a family, and watch *The Dick Van Dyke Show* together. Every time Dick tripped over something, my father would rock with laughter. He had an easy laugh, open and full and light. He was so easy to talk to and to be around. We all had a good time together. We took a vacation every summer. My father did all the driving, and my mother prepared all the food for the car.

"One trip to Dallas sticks in my mind to this day. For some odd reason, I remember seeing really big spiders; but, what really stuck with me was the sight of Black people living in 'share cropper shacks' because of racism. Our parents wanted us to see the world first hand, good or bad.

"In 1964, Our parents took us to The New York World's Fair. While far-off places gave me glorious experiences , I enjoyed our most common type of vacation — a lake trip. You see, we took the majority of our vacations either at Fox Lake in Indiana, or Benton Harbor, Michigan. We usually stayed for about two weeks on those trips, and the memories are very precious to me.

"When he was at home, my father never just sat around and did nothing. He always had little jobs going. He painted and kept everything in good repair. As a matter of fact, he even took an upholstery course once. After completing the course, he recovered every piece of furniture in the house. I remember him saying that when he retired, he wanted to open his own little upholstery shop. I can close my eyes and still see him stitching fabric with a big, curved needle in his hand. One thing was certain, he was not a sedentary person.

"My father kept the books for The Alpha Home, an African-American retirement home in Indianapolis. He was especially gifted with numbers, a talent my relatives told me that he inherited from his mother. Oh, how my father *loved* his mother.

"When Dad was in school, my grandmother participated in local Shelbyville politics. Because of her involvement, she was one of the first 'women of color' to work at the sprawling U.S. Army Finance Center, located at Fort Benjamin Harrison, on the east edge of Indianapolis. So, in her own way, she was a pacesetter, just like Dad.

"Most people remember my father as a basketball player, but he was very smart in so many other areas. To be truthful, my parents were both exceptionally smart, and amazingly, very much alike. Both of them were high achievers, both of them were self-motivated, and both of them loved their mothers and valued 'family.'

" As far as homework was concerned, no one mandated that we do it. We knew that we were expected to do it, so we just did it — without question. Doing our homework was as natural to us as taking a breath.

"My father loved sports — all sports, and he loved games. He instinctively recognized the value of playing games as a fun adjunct to formal schooling. He taught us to play checkers, chess, billiards, badminton, Ping-Pong, and 'putt-putt' golf. What's more, he played to win. He never just 'let' us win. And he never lost. When he played a sport — any sport — he played to win.

"He was a real competitor, a 'cut you down with a look' competitor. I can see that in my brother and sister. Billy and Judy both inherited that Garrett 'competitive edge.' Dad 'went all out' when it came to any kind of competition, but, he managed to instill a high level of confidence in all of us at a very early age.

"When he taught me to ride my bicycle, the scene was the picture of everyday Americana. I pedaled madly and he ran behind me, his hand on the fender to make sure I didn't fall. I still remember how funny it felt to look back and to see my six-foot-two inch father running behind my little bicycle. All of a sudden, I was shocked and surprised to realize that I was riding all by myself. I was thrilled at my accomplishment, but I took great comfort in knowing that my father was right there behind me. He was there to keep me safe.

"My sisters and I swam competitively. We were the very first Black family in our city to swim in open competition. During our weekends at 'away meets,' organizers scheduled preliminaries from Saturday morning through early afternoon and the finals for Sunday afternoon. Given that timetable, we had Saturday evening and Sunday until after lunch all to ourselves. Dad made it a practice check out the area. Then, he and mother either took us bowling or to a movie. We saw a lot of movies as a family.

"My sister, Tina, and I learned to play the piano, but she had far more talent than I. In fact, in addition to being a fine pianist, she became quite an accomplished cellist.

"My father loved us so much. He took an active role in our young lives. He was even an advocate and defender, if we needed him in that capacity. But, beyond that, he had another clear strength. His tremendous influence surfaced vividly when we made our eventual career choices.

"Our Dad was never a sexist. He never conveyed a message about 'girls' or what girls 'could or could not do.' In his eyes, we could do anything we wanted to do in life, if we worked hard. This is evident in our lives today. All three of us girls chose careers in what were considered, at the time, male-dominated professions. Moreover, I feel that my career in the ministry directly links to my father.

"The mainstay of my career choice is my father's personal spirituality. He was very active at our church, and I can remember waiting after services while he counted the money from the morning offering. But, more than anything else, I remember so clearly how he prayed.

"Most little children learn to pray at their bedsides. That's such a traditional thing. My father prayed on his knees every night before he went to bed. That image is stamped in my mind. He didn't pore over church teachings to us. Nothing was spoken. The message was much more powerful than words alone. My father taught faith by pure example.

"My father was extremely easy to be around. Neither of my parents were strict parents. They pursued their careers and fully supported one another. I didn't realize until I was an adult that other people experienced a far different home life. I thought that everyone lived in a home where they parents worked as a team. All things considered, I'd say that our home was extremely 'child friendly.'

"My father was funny. He was handsome. He was extremely confident, yet he was so humble. He was the nicest man I ever knew. As a minister, I never evangelize with people. I try to portray my faith as self-evident — as my father did. I learned a lot from him. His guidance has served me well.

"No matter what my father was doing around our home, he drew us to him. If he were mopping the floor, we'd stand at the edge of the room and talk to him. If he were mowing the grass, we'd pick up sticks or rake the leaves for him. We never felt in the way. We felt as if we were a part of things. He shared his life with us. I am grateful for that. I loved him dearly.

"I never understood why he had to die. It was too much for me to process at that age. Death is a terrible burden to a child, especially when it comes in such a shocking manner and to such a young parent.

"I know that we talked to one another, but I was just a child. More than anything, I wish that I could talk to him today. There are so many things I want to ask him. There are so many old boyfriends that I want him to intimidate! There are countless episodes I want to share with him. He bequeathed me such a rich life. There are so many gifts for which I wish to thank him.

"I know, in my heart, that not every little girl had a father like mine. I am richer for my experience, and I am blessed. My father was the finest man I ever knew. He loved my mother, my sisters, my brother, and me, and I know he loved God. My father was a truly virtuous man."

William "Billy" Guess Garrett – Crispus Attucks High School, 1983; B. A., Youth Agency Administration, The University of Indianapolis, 1991; Admissions Director and Head Basketball Coach, Providence-St. Mel High School, Chicago, Illinois, 1993-2000; Assistant Basketball Coach, Siena College, Loudenville, New York, 2000; Assistant Basketball Coach, Seton Hall University, Newark, New Jersey, 2001; married; father of one son, William Leon Garrett II, age six:

"My father believed he could do anything, but he felt he didn't have to let you know that. Most of the things I do, I learned from my father — how to pass the ball…how to make good decisions… how not to be afraid of being a champion… how not to have any fear of failure…. His humility was one of his strongest attributes. He had the right temperament to break the color barrier. He was aggressive, but not confrontational. Every time I see a documentary about Jackie Robinson, I notice his character attributes are similar to those of my father.[39]

"Basketball was a vehicle for my father's life. Basketball provided him a better life, and, in turn, it provided a better life for his family. To me, my father's legacy is one of hard work and commitment. His words remain clear in mind. 'If you have talent, don't let it consume you. To improve your life, use your talent, don't let it use you.' He taught me to put God first in my life, and he stressed that I remain humble, above all else.

"Character was key to his life. He had a unique perspective on character and how people perceive it. In his words, 'Talent is what you do when others are looking at you. Character is what you do when no one is looking at you.'

"He had the ability to make the best out of any situation. He was absolutely determined that I have a basketball court in the backyard when I was young. One day, he told me he was going to make me one. Well, I was just a little kid at the time, so I thought he meant that he was going to make a court like they had at the 'Y" — inside. I figured that he couldn't do that.

"Back then, stores didn't sell complete goals; they just sold rims and nets. For that reason, most fathers simply nailed a backboard on the family garage. That wasn't good enough for my father. He measured the height of the garage and told me that a rim nailed to it would not be the right height. It would be much too low. After doing some paperwork, he went to the lumberyard. There, he bought a stack of 2x4's, plywood, and nails. First, he nailed the 2x4's together to form a sturdy pole. It looked very big to me.

"Instead of burying the pole in a cement-filled hole, Dad made a heavy base of concrete blocks. He left a small space among the blocks and wedged the pole firmly into the center. Next, he cut a backboard out of plywood and attached it to a frame made from the remainder of the 2x4's. When he finally mounted the rim on the backboard, it measured exactly ten feet. I was completely amazed. The goal my father made for me was really impressive. It was regulation size, too, and he made it just for me.

"I can't begin to explain how that made me feel. I really

got a lot of enjoyment out of that basketball court. We spent a lot of time out there together, the two of us. He was an incredible father.

"When he taught me how to do a lay up, he used a positive reinforcement technique. I was supposed to start with my left foot and shoot with my right hand. If I failed to execute any part of the moves correctly, he simply blocked my shot. That got my attention!

"I kept trying until I got it right. I know now that his method of teaching not only instilled the basics of basketball in me, but it also gave me a lot of confidence when I played with my friends. The same thing went for a jump shot. When I began to try that move, I would throw the ball from my shoulder.

"He stopped me and explained that I must start from the top of my forehead. He told me to think about what I was going to do and then concentrate on doing it right. Fundamentals were the core of his coaching method. Today, I use those same tactics with my own son.

"Like my sisters, I swam competitively. Our whole family enjoyed the swim meets. My mother was the coach in that department, but my father helped me into my swim trunks and he watched me. My parents gave us all a lot of support in our athletic pursuits. Above all, they taught us to do our best and not to gloat. Talent and merit speak for themselves. Today, when I coach basketball, I use my father's methods with my own players. I owe him a lot."

Betty Guess Garrett Inskeep – Broadway High School, 1945; B. S. Physical Education, Indiana University, 1950; Master's Degree in Physical Education, Indiana University, 1954; Harry E. Wood High School Coach and teacher 1956-

Hetty Gray

1968; M .A. Degree in Counseling, Indiana University, Bloomington, 1969; Counselor, Kennedy Middle School, 1969-1970; High School Counselor, Shortridge High School, 1972-72; Dean of Girls, Shortridge High School until it closed in 1980 (In 1981, the school was converted to Shortridge Middle School.); retired, Indianapolis, Indiana:

"Bill visited this earth a brief moment. During that brief moment, he sprinkled the earth and all of its people with peace, joy, and, especially, love. His presence on earth greatly enriched it in many uncharted ways. Bill was grounded in an unshakable faith, a strong spirit, and a harbored resiliency beyond human understanding.

"I always felt, and experienced, in all our shared life experiences, the reassurance of being lovingly nurtured, comforted, and protected. His family rested in a cocoon — a miraculous ark of safety, surrounded by his sea of enthusiasm."

"...having been clothed...with compassion, kindness, humility, meekness, and patience." Colossians 3:12.

Epilogue

Indiana's love affair with basketball is legendary. Hoosiers have lived and died basketball for well over a century. Indiana's one class, winner take all, high school tournament titillated hometown crowds and awed out of state fans for decades but it also inspired the movie *Hoosiers*.

MGM released the popular film November 14, 1986. David Anspaugh not only directed screen veterans Gene Hackman, Barbara Hershey, and Dennis Hopper — he also directed real live Hoosiers. Among them were Ray Crowe, who played Hackman's opposing coach in the final contest and Indiana sportscaster Tom Carnegie, who played the PA Announcer during the championship game. However entertaining, the film could not begin to address the racial tension of the 1950s.

One of the major, yet unsung, changes was the smooth integration among the races in the smaller cities and towns. Shelbyville epitomized that change, because it brought Negroes and whites together in the seventh grade long before the total integration in all twelve grades.

In March of 1975, Shelbyville named its high school gymnasium for a favorite son. The William L. Garrett Gymnasium honors a man who brought honor and pride to the entire community. Inside the arena, just above the main entry, hangs a huge color photograph of the 1947 Indiana High School

State Champion Shelbyville Golden Bears.

There, among his treasured friends and beloved coaches, Bill's smile will never fade...his eyes will never lose their sparkle...his enthusiasm will never wane...his legend will never end.... So long as there is a Shelbyville youngster who picks up a basketball for the first time, Bill's influence will live on, because tradition, and heritage, will not let it die.

This remarkable tribute to Bill not only shows the depth of the love of a community for one of its own, but it also reinforces the meaning of "home" in hometown. Home, in this case, connotes far more than simply a physical location, home is a feeling...home is pride...home is memory...home is love...

Bill Garrett's life exemplified the very best in America. He lived his life in a manner reminiscent of a Norman Rockwell painting or an Aaron Copeland suite. His was a life void of audacity, yet sated with startling contrasts. Tender, but tenacious, witty yet wise, he exuded the pure, incorruptible persona that many respected, yet one they could not equal.

Even as a child, Bill competed with a sense of fairness more often seen in a much older individual. As he grew, maturing into a talented teenage athlete, he never answered the pitiless shouts of bigots with words. Instead, he responded with an explosion of talent that put to rest any question about either his talent or his poise.

As an adult, he served his country without hesitation. He viewed every job, whether on a factory assembly line, in a classroom, on a basketball court, or behind a counselor's desk, as an open-ended opportunity for service to others. Staunch and unwavering, he consistently put others before himself.

In his book, sportsmanship bested showmanship. Those who knew him best respected him as a man who embodied the triumph of selflessness over self. His composure and humility not only endeared him to his tens of thousands of fans, but also it also forged a bond with those people who were fortunate enough to know him as a teacher, a coach, and an advisor. There is no way to measure the love that his friends and family held for him.

To Bill Garrett, victory equated to team achievement. He never focused on individual accomplishment, most of all , his own. It is small wonder that his legacy far outstrips his athletic statistics. For, in the end, where can one measure the effects of mentoring and guidance? No actuary calculates such achievements. Yet, their sum total glistens in every life that Bill touched in his forty-five years.

Additional Posthumous Honors

The Indiana Basketball Hall of Fame inducted Bill Garrett in 1974.* In another parallel of two lives, Dr. Herman B Wells delivered the acceptance speech on Bill's behalf. Of course, many of his comments duplicate facts included in this book, yet the following excerpts impart the strong bond that the two of them shared.

"If ever a player deserved the title of 'Mr. Basketball,' this young man did. He led Shelbyville's Golden Bears to the State Championship in 1947 and earned the title, 'Mr. Basketball.' This three sport letter winner then moved to Indiana University where, under Coach Branch McCracken, he twice gained All Big Ten Honors, and in 1951, was named All American by both *Look Magazine* and *The Sporting News*. After three years as a player for The Harlem Globetrotters, this tall and talented athlete moved to Crispus Attucks High School, where he stayed for twelve years, ten as a coach and two as an athletic director. He was named The Indiana High School Coach of the Year in 1959, as he took his Tigers to the State Championship.

"It's most unusual for a man to be both a State Champion as a player and as a coach. During his years at Attucks, he continued his education and earned a Master's Degree at Butler University and also a Guidance Certificate in the same graduate school.

"…We salute a great champion, as a team player, coach, and a teacher, William L. 'Bill' Garrett."

In 1984, The Indiana University Hall of Fame inducted Bill into its ranks. His name joined those of several distinguished men who were pivotal to his groundbreaking career at Indiana University. Among these were 1982 inductees, IU Athletic Director Zora Clevenger, and IU Head Basketball Coach Branch McCracken, who both worked behind the scenes before Bill came to Indiana. In addition, the 1983 inductees included Ernie Andres, Assistant Coach under Branch McCracken.

Coincidentally, in 1984, The IU Hall of Fame inducted Herman B Wells in the same ceremony as Bill Garrett. Once more, the two men's lives meshed in a field of honor. Their reputations, their personal lives, and their careers rested on a firm foundation in which integrity and character were the cornerstones. In retrospect, their distinctly different lives shared elements that deserve the highest possible recognition.

In the end, one can pay no greater tribute to any man than to acclaim him to have lived a good life — a life lived more for others than for self.

*In 1974, The Indiana Basketball Hall of Fame Awards Banquet was held in the fall, after Bill's death. Today, these annual ceremonies are held in March.

Endnotes:

1 Wilson, William E. *Indiana: A History*. Bloomington, Indiana: Indiana University Press, 1966, p. 87.

2 Oldham County Historical Society, LaGrange, Kentucky.

3 Quarles, Benjamin. *The Negro in the Civil War*. New York: The Da Capo Press, 1953, p. 87.

4 Ibid., p. 193.

5 McFadden, Marian. *Biography of a Town*. Shelbyville, Indiana: Tippecanoe Press, 1968, p. 121.

6 McFadden, p. 183.

7 McFadden, pp. 202-204

8 *The Shelby Republican*, August 19, 1902.

9 Wilson, p. 121.

10 McFadden, p. 292.

11 McFadden, p. 256

12 Hamilton, Ron. *The Shelbyville News*, October 4, 2000.

13 McFadden, p. 313.

14 Schwomeyer, Herbert. Personal interview.

15 *The Shelbyville Democrat*, March 24, 1947.

16 *The Shelbyville Democrat*, March 24, 1947.

17 *The Indianapolis Star-News*, March 24, 1947.

18 Schwomeyer, Herb. *Hoosier Hysteria: A History of Indiana High School Boys Single Class Basketball*. Greenfield, Indiana: Mitchell-Fleming Printing, Inc., 1997 Edition.

19 *The Shelbyville Democrat*, March 27, 1947.

20 International News Service, March 27, 1947.

21 Wells, Herman B.* *Being Lucky*. Bloomington, Indiana: The Indiana University Press, 1980, p. 216-17.

22 Ibid., p. 217.

23 Ibid., pp. 217-18.

24 Wells, Herman B.,* p. 216

25 "IU Breaks Basketball 'Color' Barrier in 1947." DeAnna Hines, March 7, 1986.

26 Mary Jo McCracken. *The Indiana Daily Student*. March 7, 1986.

27 Harlem Globetrotters International, Inc. *The Harlem Globetrotters' Incredible 75 Year Journey*. Phoenix, Arizona: unspecified publisher, pp. 4-5. (Archivist: Govoner Vaughn), not dated.

28 Ibid.

29 Inskeep, Betty Garrett. Personal interview.

30 Bodenhamer, David J. and Barrows, Robert G. *The Encyclopedia of Indianapolis*. Bloomington, Indiana: The Indiana University Press, 1994, p. 484.

31 Ibid., p. 531.

32 Bodenhamer, p. 484.

33 Ibid.

34 Indiana Basketball Hall of Fame Inductee Database, 2001.

35 Ibid.

36 Ibid.

37 Indiana University Media Relations Office, 2001.

38 Ibid.

39 *Indiana Daily Student*. "IU's Jackie Robinson: Hoosier breaks Big Ten color line." April 17, 1997, p. 16.

*Chancellor Wells' name does not include a period after his middle initial. Periods are only for format.

Bibliography

Boetcker, Reverend William J. H. *Picturesque Shelbyville*. Indianapolis, Indiana: Levey Brothers & Company, 1903.

History of Shelby County, 1887. Chicago: Brandt & Fuller, 1887.

DePrimio, Pete and Rick Notter. *Hoosier Handbook: Stories, Stats, and Stuff About IU Basketball*. Wichita Kansas: Midwest Sports Publications, 1995.

McFadden, Marian. *Biography of a Town*. Shelbyville, Indiana: Tippecanoe Press, 1968.

Quarles, Benjamin. *The Negro in the Civil War*. New York: DaCapo Press, 1953.

Schwomeyer, Herb. *Hoosier Hysteria, Ninth Edition*. Greenfield, Indiana: Mitchell-Fleming Printing, Inc., 1977.

Selected Articles on Indiana Basketball. *The Indiana Daily Student*. Bloomington, Indiana: The Indiana University Main Library Microforms Department, 1947-51.

The Arbutus, Volumes 56, 57, 58, and 59 (1949-1951). Bloomington, Indiana: Indiana University Press, 1949-51.

The Squib, 1946 and 1947. Shelbyville, Indiana: The Shelbyville High School.

Hetty Gray

Wells, Herman B*, Chancellor of Indiana University. *Being Lucky: Reminiscences and Reflections.* Indianapolis and Bloomington: The Indiana University Press, 1980.

Wilson, William E. *Indiana: A History*. Bloomington, Indiana: Indiana University Press, 1966.

*Chancellor Wells used no period after his middle initial. The letter "B" is actually his middle name. The period here is used for format purposes only.